Cambridge E

Elements in the Philosophy
edited by
Desmond Hogan
Princeton University
Howard Williams
University of Cardiff
Allen Wood
Indiana University

KANT'S IDEAS OF REASON

Katharina T. Kraus
Johns Hopkins University

Shaftesbury Road, Cambridge CB2 8EA, United Kingdom

One Liberty Plaza, 20th Floor, New York, NY 10006, USA

477 Williamstown Road, Port Melbourne, VIC 3207, Australia

314–321, 3rd Floor, Plot 3, Splendor Forum, Jasola District Centre, New Delhi – 110025, India

103 Penang Road, #05-06/07, Visioncrest Commercial, Singapore 238467

Cambridge University Press is part of Cambridge University Press & Assessment, a department of the University of Cambridge.

We share the University's mission to contribute to society through the pursuit of education, learning and research at the highest international levels of excellence.

www.cambridge.org
Information on this title: www.cambridge.org/9781009507325

DOI: 10.1017/9781009024273

© Katharina T. Kraus 2025

This publication is in copyright. Subject to statutory exception and to the provisions of relevant collective licensing agreements, no reproduction of any part may take place without the written permission of Cambridge University Press & Assessment.

When citing this work, please include a reference to the DOI 10.1017/9781009024273

First published 2025

A catalogue record for this publication is available from the British Library

ISBN 978-1-009-50732-5 Hardback
ISBN 978-1-009-01109-9 Paperback
ISSN 2397-9461 (online)
ISSN 2514-3824 (print)

Cambridge University Press & Assessment has no responsibility for the persistence or accuracy of URLs for external or third-party internet websites referred to in this publication and does not guarantee that any content on such websites is, or will remain, accurate or appropriate.

Kant's Ideas of Reason

Elements in the Philosophy of Immanuel Kant

DOI: 10.1017/9781009024273
First published online: February 2025

Katharina T. Kraus
Johns Hopkins University

Author for correspondence: Katharina T. Kraus, katharina-kraus@gmx.de

Abstract: This Element introduces Kant's ideas of reason, focussing on the ideas of theoretical reason in the study of nature. It offers a novel interpretation that shows how such ideas as the soul, the world-whole, and God provide a regulative orientation for coping with human perspectival situatedness in the world. This perspectivalist interpretation reconciles two interpretive tendencies: a realist reading, according to which ideas refer to real things independent of the human mind, and a fictionalist reading, according to which ideas are heuristic fictions without reference to anything real. The perspectivalist interpretation recognizes two functions of ideas: first, ideas outline domains of possible objects, thus presenting the human mind with contexts of intelligibility in which the cognition of objects can be meaningful at all. Second, ideas project an ultimate reality as a *focus imaginarius*, which serves as a normative ideal for evaluating the success of human inquiries into nature.

This Element also has a video abstract: www.cambridge.org/EPIKKraus_abstract

Keywords: ideas of reason, intelligibility, theoretical reason, perspectivalism, truth evaluation

© Katharina T. Kraus 2025

ISBNs: 9781009507325 (HB), 9781009011099 (PB), 9781009024273 (OC)
ISSNs: 2397-9461 (online), 2514-3824 (print)

Contents

	Introduction	1
1	Ideas of Theoretical Reason	4
2	The Two Functions of Reason in Human Cognition	23
3	Kant's Visual Metaphors: *Standpoint, Horizon,* and *Focus Imaginarius*	31
4	The Perspectivalist Interpretation: The Horizon of Human Experience	38
5	The Perspectivalist Interpretation: Ultimate Reality As *Focus Imaginarius*	54
	Conclusion	66
	List of Abbreviations	69
	References	70

Introduction

Ideas of reason (*Ideen der Vernunft*) are a central element of Kant's Critical philosophy. In the *Critique of Pure Reason* (1781/1787), Kant leaves no doubt that '[a]ll our cognition starts from the senses (*Sinne*), goes from there to the understanding (*Verstand*), and ends with reason (*Vernunft*)' (A298/B355) and that 'all human cognition begins with intuitions (*Anschauungen*), goes from there to concepts (*Begriffen*), and ends with ideas (*Ideen*)' (A702/B730). Ideas of reason are concepts of totalities or unconditioned wholes that play a crucial role in all areas of Kant's transcendental philosophy: for example, the idea of the systematic unity of nature in his theory of science, the ideas of freedom and the highest good in his moral philosophy, the idea of the sublime in his aesthetics, the idea of natural purposiveness in his account of life, and the idea of an original contract in his political philosophy. In general, ideas of reason provide normative guidance or regulative orientation to human activities, such as theoretical cognition or moral deliberation, that goes beyond what is accessible to the human senses. Yet it has remained controversial what kind of representation Kant's ideas of reason are and what their legitimate use consists in. This Element is primarily concerned with the ideas of *theoretical reason* and their regulative use in the study of nature.

There is a disparate set of proposals in the literature regarding the status and function of these ideas within Kant's own Critical project, as well as regarding the way in which Kant diverges from traditional conceptions of ideas.[1] Plato and various Platonists considers ideas as having two aspects. Ideas concern a kind of *reality* that is created through a divine intellect and they define a *normative standard* that gives orientation to the distinctively human ways of knowing and acting.[2] Kant, by contrast, appears to reject the claim that ideas refer to or even truthfully describe real beings or a reality that exists independently of the human mind, since such a reference would exceed the limits of human experience. Nonetheless, Kant's ideas retain their function as normative standards.[3] But in Kant's own writings both a realist and a normative strand seem present, and both strands are still alive in current interpretations.

A recent controversy concerns precisely the question of whether Kant's ideas of reason are to be understood as concepts of real beings that exist independently of the human mind and may be truthfully described by these ideas. The accounts proposed in the literature fall roughly into two groups, which can be labelled, respectively, noumenalism and fictionalism. According to *noumenalism*, ideas are

---

[1] Kant himself invokes a comparison with Plato's notion of idea (see A313/B370–A317/B374; A568/B596–A569/B597).
[2] See Gerson (2013).   [3] See Rohlf (2010, 201–202).

'concepts of real things' (A643/B671) that refer to what Kant calls things-in-themselves. Despite the impossibility of cognizing such things, they can be classified as *noumena*, that is, objects of reason, insofar as they are denoted by ideas. Any legitimate use of ideas therefore involves a commitment to the existence of such real things. Such an existential commitment is often understood as a kind of taking-to-be-true of certain judgements that these ideas give rise to.[4] By contrast, according to *fictionalism*, ideas are 'heuristic fictions' (A771/B799) that are pragmatically useful for human activities, although they lack reference to anything real. Any legitimate use of ideas must deny an existential commitment to what these fictions describe. Fictionalism thus holds that no things exist that would correspond to these ideas and that the claims such ideas give rise to are in fact empty.[5] Following Kant's repeated claim that ideas have a real object only in their practical use, some opt for a fictionalist reading regarding the ideas of theoretical reason (in acquiring explanations and knowledge of empirical objects), but for a realist reading regarding the ideas of practical reason (in specifying conditions for moral agency).[6]

This Element focusses on the ideas of theoretical reason, especially the ideas of the soul, the world-whole, and God, and their regulative function for the empirical study of nature. The regulative use of ideas provides rules or guiding principles that give direction and regulation to the cognitive activities of the mind. To supply objectively binding rules that are more than just subjective precepts, this use seems to imply claims about an objective reality that cannot be proven empirically. Examples of such claims are that nature is systematically unified and that there is a mental substance in which all thoughts inhere. While the noumenalist accepts these claims as truths, the fictionalist considers them as heuristically useful, albeit empty fictions. Both interpretations owe an explanation for the prescriptive function of ideas in experience.

---

[4] This line of interpretation led to reappropriations of Kant's transcendental philosophy in German idealism that show a tendency towards determining the unconditioned, e.g., Fichte's (1796–1799) absolute I and Hegel's (1807) absolute idea. A growing number of Kant scholars defend the view that Kant's theory of reason entails the commitment to the existence of something unconditioned, e.g., Ameriks (2003, 2006), Hogan (2009), Pickering (2016), Stang (2016), Watkins (2016, 2019b), Proops (2021), and Schafer (2023). This commitment is often understood as a *doctrinal belief*, e.g., Chignell (2007a), Stang (2016), Schafer (2023). However, these accounts rarely explicitly address ideas of reason.

[5] This line of interpretation was famously proposed by Vaihinger (1911) and is also present in Cassirer (1999). Representatives in recent Kant scholarship include Grier (2001), Allison (2004), Dyck (2014), and McLaughlin (2014).

[6] A recent example is Willaschek (2018:254–262, 270–275). For textual evidence, see, e.g., 'Thus the principles of pure reason have objective reality in their practical use, that is, in the moral use' (A808/B836); see also Bxxx, A328/B385, A366, B431, A633/B661, A776/B804, A796/B824, and A804/B832.

This Element develops a *perspectivalist* interpretation of Kant's ideas of theoretical reason that reconciles both noumenalism and fictionalism.[7] These ideas play an indispensable role in the perspectival situatedness of human attempts to understand the world. Calling this interpretation perspectivalist does not imply that Kant's position is relativist, for example, with respect to truth or knowledge. Rather, the proposed interpretation will suggest that although our cognition is limited to a distinctively *human perspective*, it must be guided by a demanding ideal: we should strive to understand the world as it is in itself independent of the human perspective. The human perspective includes a *standpoint* from which we have experience of spatio-temporal objects and a *horizon* that defines the limits of what we can understand at all. But it is still possible – indeed, necessary – to aim at knowing the world as it may exist independently of the human mind.

The regulative use of ideas, according to the perspectivalist view, is twofold. First, it demarcates and outlines the horizon of human intelligibility within which we can make out and determine objects of experience at all – this is the world of appearances or simply nature.[8] Ideas play a heuristic role in the formation of empirical concepts and in seeking systematic explanations for empirical phenomena. Second, the regulative use of ideas projects a target world that is ultimately to be aimed at – that is the world in itself or simply things-in-themselves. Ideas thus stand in as placeholders for the ultimate reality that would make our cognition true. These projections serve as normative ideals for human inquiries. Ideas thus give us a regulative orientation for coping with our perspectival situatedness in the world in two ways. First, they present us with relevant contexts of intelligibility to guide our cognitive activities to the greatest possible systematic unity of cognition. Second, they provide us with normative standards for evaluating the success of these activities.[9]

The proposed perspectivalist view, I argue, reconciles fictionalism and noumenalism by qualifying the existential commitments in each case in important ways: Ideas play both a constructive role in structuring and conceptualizing the

---

[7] One way to reconcile these two seemingly contradictory views is to support qualified versions of each view that are compatible with each other. These qualifications may, for example, concern the nature of the existential commitment to things that ideas refer to. Noumenalism and fictionalism, as stated above, can be considered as the two opposite ends of a spectrum of views.

[8] This metaphor of a horizon has been taken up in post-Kantian philosophy, especially in phenomenology and hermeneutics in terms of the *horizon of understanding* and the *life-world* (e.g., Husserl 1900, Heidegger 1927, Gadamer 1960).

[9] Massimi (2017 and 2021) has recently developed a perspectivalist interpretation of Kant's ideas, which shares important similarities with my interpretation. A key difference concerns the fact that I distinguish between two aspects of the human perspective – the human horizon and a target world – and relatedly two functions of ideas – a content-enabling function regarding appearances and a truth-evaluative function against the background of a projected target world.

world of appearances and a realist role in directing us to a mind-independent reality. Like fictionalism, the view denies that empirical reality, or the world of appearances, can ever fully realize what the ideas describe. Unlike fictionalism, however, the view concedes that ideas also project placeholders for what would ultimately make our cognition true, independently of the human perspective we take on it. Ideas are therefore not mere fictions. Like noumenalism, the view allows at least for the possibility that real things corresponding to ideas exist. What it denies, however, unlike strong versions of noumenalism, is that ideas amount to true, assertible judgements about this mind-independent reality. On the perspectivalist view, any truth-apt, assertible judgement requires a domain in which it applies. This domain is precisely defined by an idea, but as a whole it can never itself be determined in a judgement. By contrast, both fictionalism and noumenalism, in the versions stated above, err in assuming that we can assert (or deny) the truth of certain claims about the domain as a whole, or so I argue.

Section 1 introduces Kant's conception of reason and explores *noumenalism* and *fictionalism* in more depth. Section 2 specifies the two regulative functions of reason: its semantic function in determining empirical content and its epistemic function in evaluating truth. Section 3 introduces three visual metaphors that Kant uses to illustrate the function of reason in the Appendix to the Dialectic of the first *Critique* – the metaphors of *standpoint*, *horizon*, and *focus imaginarius*. The perspectivalist reading developed in Sections 4 and 5 offers a compelling account of these metaphors. Section 4 explains how ideas characterize the human standpoint and outline the universal human *horizon* within which human subjects can make sense of their experience as truth-apt, inferential cognition of objects. Section 5 shows how ideas project an ultimate reality, albeit only as a *focus imaginarius*. This projection provides a normative standard for assessing the truth of human cognition.

1 Ideas of Theoretical Reason

When I recently observed a lion and a giraffe in a wildlife park, I wondered how much they have in common: Both, for example, are animals, need air to breathe, and suckle their offspring. At the same time, there are significant differences in their physical constitution, their way of moving, and their eating habits. According to Kant, it is our faculty of *reason* (*Vernunft*) that guides us to organize these similarities and differences, to derive further characteristics from individual observations, and to find general laws to explain them. In the *Critique of Pure Reason*, Kant therefore praises human reason as the highest of all mental faculties, but he also warns us of its 'peculiar fate': due to its very nature, reason leads us to questions and ideas that transcend its own limits, but which are nonetheless 'given to it as problems' (Avii).

To understand the nature and function of ideas of reason, we must first look at this multifaceted conception of reason. Subsection 1.1 introduces reason as the faculty for syllogistic inferences and for the generation of hypotheses according to the *Critique of Pure Reason*. Subsection 1.2 describes reason's characteristic tendency to strive for completeness, which leads to the totality of conditions and ultimately to the unconditioned. Subsection 1.3 shows how ideas of reason are formed as part of this striving for completeness. Subsection 1.4 specifies possible uses of reason and introduces the regulative use of ideas. Subsections 1.5 and 1.6 explore the two lines of interpretation that I have called *noumenalism* and *fictionalism*.

1.1 Reason As Faculty for Inference and Hypothesis Formation

In the *Critique of Pure Reason*, Kant discusses the peculiar fate of reason mainly in the Transcendental Dialectic: there, he introduces reason primarily as the *faculty of inferring*, before setting out to raise a fundamental critique of the illicit use of reason in dialectical inferences leading to transcendental illusions.[10] According to this definition, reason's most common employment is in drawing syllogistic inferences. Such *inferences of reason* connect two judgements (a major premise and a conclusion) through the mediation of a third one (the minor premise) (see A309/B366). Typically, such inferences proceed *deductively*: they start from a given, general rule (i.e., the major premise) and descend towards a specific application of that rule (i.e., the conclusion).[11] To adapt a classic example:

(Major premise)   *All human beings are mortal.*

(Minor premise)   *Xanthippe is a human being.*

(Conclusion)   *Xanthippe is mortal.*

In this deductive function, reason builds on the workings of the understanding (*Verstand*) – in its function of combining concepts (and ultimately intuitions) into judgements – and also on the deliverances of sensibility (*Sinnlichkeit*) – in

---

[10] For example, A299/B355 and A330/B386. Note that at times Kant employs the notion of 'reason in general' (e.g., A760/B788) to refer to all higher intellectual faculties, including the understanding and the power of judgement. I use 'reason' to denote the faculty in the narrow sense. The goal of the Transcendental Dialectic is to dismantle the arguments of traditional rationalist metaphysics.

[11] Kant himself uses the notion of a 'derivation' (e.g., A300/B357, FI 20:201). The set of problems his account of reason addresses can also be discussed in terms of *deductive* and *inductive reasoning*.

terms of its sensory intuitions. Reason depends on the understanding for supplying general cognitions that can be used as major premises, and on the power of judgement (*Urteilskraft*) for subsuming a more specific cognition under a general one in the minor premise.[12] Reason thus assists the understanding in gaining cognition through its 'derivation ... from principles' (A300/B357) and preserves the objective validity of the premises for the conclusion.

As such, reason appears to be 'merely subordinate' to the understanding (A305/B362): by subsuming the condition of a given cognition (in the minor premise) under a universal rule (the major premise), reason reveals a more general condition of that cognition and thereby promotes the aim of the understanding to determine an object through cognition. The example syllogism above reveals *mortality* as a more general condition of *Xanthippe* than the already known condition of *being human*.

Kant distinguishes three logical forms of syllogisms dependent on three forms the major premise can take: Following the three forms of relational judgements, the *categorical syllogism* has a categorical judgement as its major premise ('A is p'), the *hypothetical syllogism* has a hypothetical judgement as its major premise ('If A is p, then B is q'), and the *disjunctive syllogism* has a disjunctive judgement as its major premise ('A is p or A is q') (where A and B are subject terms, and p and q are predicates).[13]

Yet this deductive function also raises the question of how we can find general rules in the first place. In order to recognize a generalization, we must be provided with a set of experiences and by comparing and contrasting these experiences find observational patterns. To explain these patterns, we posit a hypothesis as the general rule that governs the observed objects. For example, if we observe the falling of several material objects, such as the dropping of an apple from a tree and the sliding of a feather to the ground, we can find a common pattern in these observations despite noticeable differences and eventually identify a general causal rule, such as Newton's law of gravitation.

Kant does not explicitly provide us with an account of *inductive* reasoning, through which one can derive a universal rule from individual cases. Nonetheless, he is familiar with the work of Francis Bacon, who first defined the method of induction as the fundamental knowledge-generating principle of the empirical sciences, as well as with David Hume's sceptical doubts regarding induction.[14] Kant occasionally addresses related issues in his account of laws of

---

[12] See also A304/B360–1. In this function, reason is also understood as 'the faculty for the determination of the particular through the general (for the derivation from principles)' (FI 20:201).

[13] See A304/B361, JL 9:121–122.

[14] For example, Bxii and A765/B793. See Bacon (1620/2012) and Hume (1748/2007).

nature, especially with respect to the search for particular empirical laws.[15] In the *Critique of the Power of Judgment*, Kant introduces the *reflecting power of judgement* to explain how to find a universal rule under which given particulars can be subsumed.[16]

In the first *Critique*, Kant still sees a fundamental role of reason in the search for general rules, namely in its *hypothetical use*, which he introduces only in the Appendix to the Dialectic. The hypothetical use is 'not such that if one judges in all strictness the truth of the universal rule assumed as a hypothesis thereby follows', but rather such use is 'only regulative, bringing unity into particular cognitions as far as possible and thereby *approximating* the rule to universality' (A647/B675). Reason in its hypothetical use generates hypotheses that generalize over what is given in experience, but it cannot guarantee the universal validity of the hypothesis as it does in the case of derivative inferences. Even though reason goes beyond immediate inferences from actual experience, it still operates within the realm of possible experience. A hypothesis can be tested in light of particular empirical cognitions and is confirmed (or at least corroborated) as a general rule, if (or as long as) no counterexample is found.[17] We may, for example, hypothesize that animals are mortal, and this hypothesis has been corroborated as a general rule, since *so far* no immortal animal has ever been discovered.[18]

By assigning the function of generating hypotheses to reason, Kant reverses the direction in which reason operates in inferences, as well as the dependence relation between reason and the understanding. Reason no longer descends from the universal validity of a rule established by the understanding to a more specific application of that rule in the conclusion, as is the case in deductive

---

[15] See A664/B692; FI 20:202–204; CJ 5:237. On Kant's account of laws of nature and empirical lawlikeness, see in particular Buchdahl (1969, 1971), Massimi and Breitenbach (2017), and Watkins (2019a).

[16] See FI 20:211–212, 244; CJ 5:179–181. Some take Kant's theory of reflective judgement in the third *Critique* to replace his account of transcendental ideas in the first *Critique* (e.g., Guyer (1990)); for others, transcendental ideas still define principles for this reflective use (e.g., Allison (2004)). For discussion, see Makkreel (1990), and with respect to empirical laws, see Zuckert (2007) and Massimi and Breitenbach (2017).

[17] Kant's positive account of reason in the Appendix is frequently understood to address the problem of induction (e.g., Grier 2001, Allison 2004:425–433, Sturm 2009, Massimi 2021). That the hypothetical use of reason plays a key role in Kant's account of lawfulness (in nature) and of the discovery of scientific laws is noted, e.g., by Buchdahl (1969), Rush (2000), Massimi (2017, 2021), and Willaschek (2018). The set of problems Kant addresses in the Appendix is broader than Hume's problem of induction, as Kant also considers the formation of empirical concepts, the definition of natural kinds, and the evaluation of truth (see 2.2 and 2.3).

[18] The counterfactual assumption of immortality in this example is not well defined within the domain of possible experience, since its predicate runs across a temporally infinite domain. But the hypothesis can gain more support from a biological explanation of the complex biological processes that lead to the mortality of organisms.

inferences. Rather, reason now ascends towards a more general universality than that hitherto cognized through the understanding. Reason now directs the understanding 'by opening up new paths into the infinite (the undetermined) with which the understanding is not acquainted, yet without ever being the least bit contrary to the laws of its empirical use' (A680/B708).

Even though reason, in its hypothetical use, 'prepares the field for the understanding' (A657/B685), it does not yet leave the 'field of possible empirical cognition' in an illegitimate way (A644/B672). To observe these boundaries of experience, the hypothetical use should not be exercised randomly, but in some sense purposively, namely with the purpose of enhancing the faculty of cognition by maximizing its scope and explanatory power. Kant argues that 'the hypothetical use of reason is therefore directed at the systematic unity of the understanding's cognitions' (A647/B675). This systematic unity is necessary to prove (or at least corroborate) that a hypothesis '*approximat[es]* the rule to universality', that is, can be assumed as universally valid (as far as we know) (A647/B675).[19]

Kant always conceives of reason as the 'supreme faculty of cognition', which aims to pursue the 'highest unity of thinking' (A299/B355). This highest 'unity of reason' (A302/B359) is superior to the 'unity of the understanding' (A307/B363): the latter can be fully realized in experience and is reflected in the form of unity that an empirical judgement exhibits, whereas the former goes by definition beyond any experiential grasp. Let me explain with an example.

The understanding defines kinds of unities, expressed in its pure concepts, that we can find in experiential episodes, despite the fragmentary nature of our sensible intuitions. For example, when I observe a red apple rolling off my kitchen table, I have a multitude of sensible intuitions. These intuitions present the apple to me only from a particular visual perspective. They show the front, but not the back, of the apple. They might not show every infinitesimal unit of the apple's motion either. Nonetheless, by applying the understanding's pure concepts such as *substance* and *causality* – as categories – to my sensible intuitions, I can cognize the apple as a unified object, as a substance with changing accidents and persisting through a course of motions in accordance with a causal law. This leads to empirical judgements such as <The apple is red> and <The apple is rolling off the table>.[20]

---

[19] The hypothetical use is often identified with the regulative use of reason that promotes systematic unity (e.g., Allison 2004:425–431). But this passage suggests that the hypothetical use presupposes such a regulative use (see 5.1). Hume's assumption of the uniformity of nature, which is required for his sceptical solution to the problem of induction, can be seen as a special case of the assumption of systematic unity that Kant calls for (on this point, see also Allison 2004:425–430). That the hypothetical use is crucial for science, conceived as a system, is further discussed in the Doctrine of Method (A832ff./B860ff.). See Buchdahl (1969), Kitcher (1986), and Sturm (2009).

[20] I use < ... > to indicate the content of a concept or judgement.

Hence, the understanding's categories, such as substance and causality, give rules for synthesizing intuitions into specific kinds of unities. The resulting cognitions exhibit these unities defined by the understanding.

Reason, however, is not satisfied with singular cognitions. By its nature, reason keeps asking for further and further conditions of the apple. It asks, for example, about the condition of why the apple rolled off my kitchen table, but also why the apple ended up on my kitchen table in the first place, why it came into being, which biochemical processes led to its existence, and perhaps also why it has become an object of my culinary preferences. This quest of reason seems to come to an end only when reason has completely determined the apple. But in this quest for completeness, reason seeks a kind of unity 'that can never come forth in experience' (A765/B793). Reason, therefore, runs the risk of transcending the bounds of sense. Most of the Transcendental Dialectic is therefore devoted to uncovering these transgressions of reason. But why does reason pursue this 'unity of reason in appearances' (A326/B383) at all, although we cannot experience such unity? Can such a pursuit serve a constructive purpose?

1.2 The Totality of Conditions and the Unconditioned

Reason has a natural tendency to seek *completeness*, namely the totality of conditions to a given conditioned.[21] This tendency is already implied in its basic function in inferential reasoning, since the central point of an inference is to reveal a more general condition, for example, the governing law, of a given cognition and its object. Already in its harmless use in hypothesis generation, reason seeks to move beyond the rules established by the understanding. But reason strives towards the totality of conditions. The complete set of conditions, if available, would fully determine an individual thing. Reason thus seeks a complete and thoroughgoing determination of things in all their properties, including possible ones (A571/B579).

Kant explains the striving for completeness in terms of an iteration of syllogisms in an '*ascending series*', that is, a series of so-called 'prosyllogisms' (A331/B388, also A307/B364). Each prosyllogism reveals a yet more general condition for the premise of the preceding syllogism.[22] In our classic example (concerning *Xanthippe*), the next prosyllogism would have the previous major

---
[21] *Completeness* is highlighted as a central feature of (universal human) reason, for instance, by Allison (2004:423–448) and Willaschek (2018:158, 160).
[22] On prosyllogisms, see Willaschek (2018:49–53, 56–58) and Watkins (2019b).

premise that *all human beings are mortal* as its conclusion and reveal a yet more general condition. It could, for example, run as follows:

(Major premise)   *All animals are mortal.*

(Minor premise)   *All human beings are animals.*

(Conclusion)   *All human beings are mortal.*

The *whole series* of prosyllogisms results not in another conditioned cognition, but in the totality of premises, that is, the *totality of conditions* for a given conditioned cognition. In light of any given cognition, reason is 'necessitated to regard the series of conditions in an ascending line as completed and given in their totality' (A332/B388). Why is reason so necessitated? To answer this question, we have to turn to the intrinsic principles of reason itself and hence to *pure reason*, that is, reason in its *pure use* in abstraction from any (sensible or logical) content supplied by subordinated faculties (A305/B362ff.).

The first principle that reason intrinsically follows is the *logical maxim* 'to find the unconditioned for conditioned cognitions of the understanding, with which its unity will be completed' (A307/B364). This maxim is a subjectively valid 'logical prescript' that guides reason's regressive employment in an ascending series of inferences (A309/B365).[23] Yet this logical maxim raises the concern that it may only be properly applicable under the assumption that something unconditioned must exist that stops the regressive inquiry. This could be, for example, an initial unconditioned condition that started the series (e.g., the beginning of the universe in time) or something unconditioned that underlies the whole series (e.g., the noumenal character that grounds the whole series of a person's actions). Searching for the totality of conditions and ultimately for the unconditioned would be reasonable only if we assumed that these actually existed.[24]

The logical maxim therefore seems to imply a second principle, the *supreme principle of pure reason*: It appears that if the logical maxim is to be meaningful and instructive for human reason at all, then one must also 'assume that when the conditioned is given, then so is the whole series of conditions subordinated one to the other, which is itself unconditioned, also given' (A307-8/B364).[25] This supreme principle would be the candidate for the first *synthetic* principle of pure reason. It is synthetic since it reaches beyond the analytic relations between cognitions given through the understanding to something unconditioned.

---

[23] For an excellent discussion of the logical maxim, see Willaschek (2018:46–70).

[24] Arguments to this effect can be found, for example, in Pickering (2016) and Watkins (2019b).

[25] For excellent discussions of the supreme principle of pure reason and its relation to the logical maxim, see Willaschek (2018:71–126) and Schafer (2023:149–183).

Kant's Ideas of Reason

Yet this supreme principle raises an even more serious concern: since the totality of conditions and hence something unconditioned can never be encountered in experience, the supreme principle and all principles derived from it can only ever be '*transcendent*' in respect of appearances (A308/B365). Does the application of the supreme principle lead to the assumption of a *given* unconditioned?[26] Yet in the Transcendental Dialectic, Kant exposes the assumption of something unconditioned that exists 'in itself and absolutely' as a *transcendental illusion*. Such an illusion consists in the assumption that something unconditioned is given independently of the human mind but can nonetheless be determined by our categories. Kant rejects this assumption as deceptive and fallacious.[27]

1.3 The Transcendental Ideas of Reason

In its quest for completeness, pure reason becomes 'a genuine source of concepts and judgments' (A305/B362, see also A299/B355), namely of the *pure concepts of reason* or simply of *transcendental ideas* (e.g., A311/B368, A321/B378). These are 'necessary concept[s] of reason' that can be derived from reason's own iterative inferential procedure (A327/B383). These concepts are formed by 'ascending in the series of conditions' until one reaches the totality of conditions (A336/B394): 'So the transcendental concept of reason is none other than that of the *totality of conditions* to a given conditioned thing' (A322/B379). This totality is then 'explained through the concept of the unconditioned': the concept of *the unconditioned* represents the 'ground of synthesis for what is conditioned' and hence the ground of the entire series of conditions (A322/B379).

Corresponding to the three types of syllogisms – the categorical, the hypothetical, and the disjunctive syllogism – Kant distinguishes three kinds of relations that these ascending series of conditions can express: '1) the relation to the subject, 2) the relation to objects, and indeed either as appearances, or [3)] as objects of thinking in general' (A333/B390–391). These three kinds of relations lead to three classes of transcendental ideas: (1) the concept of the

---

[26] The notion 'given' in the formulation of the supreme principle is typically understood in an ontological sense as 'to exist', rather than in an epistemological sense as 'to be cognitively accessible to the human mind' (see Willaschek 2018:72–3). An ontological reading is assumed, e.g., by Grier (2001), Allison (2004), Ameriks (2003, 2006), Stang (2016:290), and Willaschek (2018:72–73). See 1.5 and 1.6.

[27] Interpreters either distinguish between transcendental illusions and fallacies or identify them, depending on how they view the status of the supreme principle. For fictionalists, transcendental illusions are unavoidable but only lead to fallacies if they are taken to be true (e.g., Grier 2001, Dyck 2014). For noumenalists, transcendental illusions consist in the a priori cognition or determination of the unconditioned and are therefore always erroneous (e.g., Schafer 2023:180).

'absolute (unconditioned) unity of the thinking subject' (A334/B391), that is, the idea of the soul or, more generally, the psychological ideas; (2) the concept of 'the absolute unity of the series of conditions of appearance' (A334/B391), that is, the idea of the world-whole or, more generally, the cosmological ideas; and (3) the concept of 'the absolute unity of the condition of all objects of thought in general' (A334/B391) or 'the idea of an All of reality (*omnitudo realitatis*)' (A575/B603), which culminates in the 'highest rational concept of a being of all beings' (*ens entium*) (A336/B393), that is, the theological idea of God.[28] Let me say a word about each.

The idea of the soul is obtained through a series of categorical syllogisms that are applied to one's representations. For each representation R_i, the thinking of R_i is predicated of a subject S_i in a categorical judgement of the form '*S* thinks *R*'. The whole series then results in the 'unconditioned ... for the categorical synthesis in a [single] subject' (A323/B379). The idea is thus the concept of 'the absolute (unconditioned) unity of the thinking subject' (A334/B391). It can be further specified by sub-concepts such as <simple thinking substance> (see A673/B701), <being endowed with a fundamental power>, and <being entirely distinct from a body> (see A682/B710). The idea, if it refers to something real, would represent a thinking substance in which all one's representations inhere.

An idea concerning the world-whole (in the broad sense) starts from a given appearance, runs through an infinite regression of hypothetical conditions ('If *A* is *p*, then *B* is *q*'), and finally completes the 'hypothetical synthesis of the members of a series' of appearances (A323/B379). This infinite regression results in the concept of 'the absolute unity of the series of conditions of appearance' (A334/B391). This absolute unity can be explicated in a variety of ways, for example, as the absolute unity of space or of time in the mathematical ideas of the *world* (in the narrow sense) (see A418/B446 ff.). This absolute unity can also mean the 'sum total [*Inbegriff*] of appearances' that are interconnected by causal laws, or simply *nature* (see A418/B446 n ff., also B163 and A328/B384).[29]

The idea of God is derived from the 'disjunctive synthesis of the parts in a system' (A323/B379), which leads to the concept of 'the absolute unity of the condition of all objects of thought in general' (A334/B391). The derivation procedure in this case is more complicated. It starts from the principle of thoroughgoing determination (PTD), according to which for each possible predicate either it or its negation applies to a thing (see A571/B579ff.). This

---

[28] For an account of the three classes of transcendental ideas, see Willaschek 2018:167–185.

[29] The cosmological ideas lead to antinomies in which reason develops contradictory concepts of the world (in the broad sense), e.g., as infinitely divisible and as composed of finite units, as causally determined and as allowing for free action. See Falkenburg (2020) and Howard (2022b, 2024).

can be expressed in a series of disjunctive judgements of the form '*A* is *p* or *A* is *non-p*'. Using this principle iteratively leads to 'the idea of an All of reality (*omnitudo realitatis*)' (A575/B603), that is, a reality in which all things are completely determined. This idea is then explained through the 'concept of a being of all beings' (*ens entium*) (A336/B393), or the concept of the highest being (i.e., '*ens realissimum*') (A576/B604), or simply the idea of God.

These three classes of transcendental ideas should not be confused with other ideas of reason such as '*pure earth, pure water, pure air*' (A646/B674). Like the transcendental ideas, these ideas are concepts of the 'form of a whole of cognition' (A645/B673). But they cannot be derived from the nature of reason itself, that is, from its forms of syllogisms. Rather, they arise by considering some empirical results in a particular area of nature and they serve to 'question nature' to find more lawful connections in that area (A645/B673). They function like idealized models in science. For example: 'one reduces all materials to earths (mere weight, as it were), to salts and combustibles (as force), and finally to water and air as vehicles (machines, as it were, by means of which the aforementioned operate), in order to explain the chemical effects of materials in accordance with the idea of a mechanism' (A646/B674).[30]

In sum, reason's characteristic inferential procedures give rise to transcendental ideas. These ideas express the *totality of conditions* for a given conditioned cognition. In turn, these totalities are 'explained' by concepts of something unconditioned (A322/B379). For example, the totality of conditions of a representation is explained by the concept of the absolute subject; the totality of conditions of a spatial entity is explained by the concept of absolute space. As concepts of absolute wholes, ideas cannot have 'congruent object[s] ... given in the senses' (A327/B383), so that their use naturally leads beyond the boundaries of experience. But what legitimate use could these ideas still have, and in what sense could they have a *transcendental* status with respect to empirical cognition?[31] Before considering the answers that noumenalist and fictionalist interpretations give to these questions (in 1.5 and 1.6, respectively), I introduce the regulative use of transcendental ideas.

1.4 Is the Regulative Use of Ideas a Real Use of Reason?

A central question is whether reason itself can provide insight into objects of cognition or even into things-in-themselves. That is, does reason have a *real use*? Kant distinguishes between a logical and a real use for both the understanding and

---

[30] On the function of these ideas in science, see Massimi (2017, 2021) and Spagnesi (2022, 2023a, 2023b).

[31] Kant also speaks of these ideas as 'transcendental presupposition[s]' (A651/B679, A678/B706) and 'transcendental principle[s]' (A650/B678, see also A663/B691).

reason. Logical use is the *mind-to-mind* application of a faculty relating mental or representational items to one another (from Greek *logos*, meaning *word, thought*, or *principle*). Real use is a *mind-to-world* application relating mental or representational items to objects or things in the world (from Latin *res*, meaning *thing*). For example, in its logical use, the understanding relates different concepts in a judgement, whereas in its real use, it applies concepts to sensible intuitions and hence makes judgments about objects of experience. In the Transcendental Analytic, Kant offers complex arguments that (and how) the real use of the understanding provides a priori transcendental principles of experience. But he is far more hesitant about reason: in fact, the Transcendental Dialectic deconstructs the rationalist attempts to derive insights about the reality of things from reason. But is there really no *legitimate real use* of reason over and above its logical use in formal syllogisms that abstract from all content?

Let us refine the taxonomy of uses of reason in comparison with the understanding. So far, reason, as the *faculty of inferring* has two kinds of uses, the *derivational (or deductive) use* and the *hypothetical (or inductive) use*. In these uses, reason relates directly to cognitions provided by the understanding. In other passages, reason is introduced as the *faculty of principles* or, more precisely, as the 'faculty of the unity of the rules of understanding under principles' (A302/B359). In this definition, reason is considered in its *pure use*, in abstraction from any content given through the understanding. Nonetheless, the understanding itself now constitutes an 'object for reason' (A664/B692): 'pure reason is never related directly to objects, but instead to concepts of them given by the understanding' (A335/B392). How does reason apply to 'concepts' or 'rules' of the understanding?

Three distinctions apply to both faculties, the understanding and reason: the distinctions (1) between a *logical* and a *real* use, (2) between an *immanent* and a *transcendent* use, and (3) between a *constitutive* and a *regulative* use.

(1) The distinction between *logical* and *real* use depends on the kind of mental item the faculty is applied to. A faculty operates on representations either in abstraction from their relation to objects or under explicit consideration of their reference to objects or things (see A299/B355). The *logical use* concerns only the logical relations among representations 'abstract[ing] from all content of cognition' (A299/B355). The logical use of the understanding combines concepts within a judgement in accordance with the forms of judgement (i.e., the 'logical functions' of the understanding, see A69ff./B94ff.). The logical use of reason combines judgements within a syllogism, in accordance with the three forms of inferences (i.e., the categorical, the hypothetical, and the disjunctive, see A299/B355 and

A303ff./B359ff.). The real use, by contrast, considers the relation the representations have to their objects.

(2) Within this *real use* we can distinguish different kinds of objects or kinds of reality that a faculty aims at. An *immanent* use concerns only objects within the 'boundaries of experience' (*Erfahrungsgrenze*) (Bxxiv, A296/B352–353, A637/B665), that is, appearances. A *transcendent* use is not limited by experience, but transcends the bounds of sense and potentially aims at things-in-themselves (see A296/B352, A637/B665, A643/B671). Kant accepts only the immanent use of the categories of the understanding for appearances as legitimate. But if the categories are taken to determine real things beyond the bounds of experience, we engage in an illegitimate 'misuse' (A296/B352) of them.[32] His critique of rationalist metaphysics rejects such transcendent use.

(3) A use can come with different *kinds of necessity (or validity)*. A *constitutive* use defines conditions that are strictly necessary (and therefore universally valid) for a representation to be of a particular type. A merely *regulative* use specifies conditions for a type of representation that are *not* strictly necessary for the type, but conducive to approximating universal validity. These are conditions we should seek to satisfy, though we may never be able to do so completely.[33]

The categories of the understanding have a constitutive use with regard to experience because they establish strictly necessary conditions for a representation to count as experience, or empirical cognition. For example, the relational categories, such as substantiality and causality, are strictly necessary for the experience of a substance with causal powers. However, the relational categories are only regulative regarding the intuitions involved: they are not strictly necessary for us to have an intuition, but they give rules for synthesizing intuitions, *if* we aim for cognition (see A664/B692 and A180/B222–223). The category of substance gives us a rule for how to combine a manifold of intuition such that a persisting substance can be distinguished from its changing accidents. Importantly, the constitutive use of the categories generates a priori real contents

---

[32] On the immanent and transcendent use of the understanding, see also A308/B365, A636/B664, A638/B666.

[33] This account is based on the following passage: 'The hypothetical use of reason ... is not properly *constitutive*, that is, not such that if one judges in *all strictness the truth of the universal rule* assumed as a hypothesis thereby follows ... Rather, this use of reason is only *regulative*, bringing unity into particular cognitions as far as possible and thereby *approximating the rule to universality*' (A647/B675, emphases added). Kant often describes the regulative use in terms of 'rules' or 'maxims' we should seek to apply, e.g., A180/B222–223, A509/B537, A666/B694, A680/B708.

of empirical cognition and thus determines the most general features of objects of possible experience, such as persistence in time.

For reason, Kant rejects a constitutive use but admits a regulative use. In the Appendix to the Dialectic, Kant identifies the 'good and consequently immanent use' of reason as the regulative use of its ideas (A643/B671). Recall that pure reason is the origin of transcendental ideas, as the pure understanding is the source of pure concepts, namely the categories. The regulative use of ideas consists in 'directing the understanding to a certain goal' (A644/B672). This goal has earlier been defined as the 'unity of reason in appearances' (A326/B383) and is now described as 'the greatest unity alongside the greatest extension' of our cognitions (A644/B672), or as 'systematic unity ... of the understanding's cognition' (A648/B676, also A647/B675). The regulative use of reason thus aims to bring systematic unity to the cognitions of the understanding. Can we construe this regulative use as a real use like that of the categories? In what sense could ideas refer to something real?

Like the understanding, the real use of reason would aim at objects or things. It would reveal not only logical entailment relations among judgements, as in its logical use, but *real conditioning relations* of cognitions. These are the relations that feature in the explanation of appearances and that correspond to relations among and within objects. Corresponding to the three forms of syllogisms – categorical, hypothetical, and disjunctive – we can distinguish three types of real conditioning relations that obtain between a cognition and its condition(s): *subsistence*, *dependence* (or causality), and *community* (or reciprocity).[34]

The real use of ideas, as concepts of absolute wholes, is often understood as the real determination of things-in-themselves (as noumena).[35] On this reading, it involves assumptions such as these: that an appearance must be grounded in the existence of an unconditioned subsistent thing, or that it must ultimately follow from an unconditioned causal power. But since, in contrast to the pure concepts of the understanding, nothing can be given to the senses that would correspond to these ideas, it is often concluded that their real use can only be transcendent and thus illegitimate. It leads precisely to the transcendental illusions Kant exposes in the Dialectic.

The question of whether or not the regulative use of ideas is a real use, and if so, to which reality it relates, divides the interpretations offered in the literature. According to what I called *noumenalism*, ideas relate to something unconditioned, and their regulative use requires a commitment to the existence of this

---

[34] This is a simplified account; the details for specific ideas, especially the cosmological ones, are more complex. See Watkins (2019b), Falkenburg (2020), Howard (2024).

[35] For example, Grier (2001), Allison (2004), Rohlf (2010), Willaschek (2018), Watkins (2019b). See fn. 36.

unconditioned reality. According to *fictionalism*, by contrast, ideas provide heuristically useful fictions, which, however, are empty, that is, without denoting anything real. I now discuss each interpretive tendency in turn and indicate potential shortcomings.

1.5 Noumenalism: Ideas As Concepts of Real Things

Noumenalism treats ideas as 'concepts of real things' (e.g., A643/B671) and assumes that they relate to what Kant calls '*noumena*' or 'beings of understanding' (B306).[36] According to its strong version, any legitimate use of ideas must involve a commitment to the existence of such real things, although we cannot have cognition of those things, since ideas cannot have corresponding intuitions. This strong version is rarely stated in the literature, and there may be good reasons for this. However, there is a growing number of views on which Kant's account of reason involves a commitment to the existence of something unconditioned.[37] This commitment, if it is explicitly discussed at all, is sometimes understood as what Kant calls '*doctrinal beliefs*' (A825/B853), a special case of the epistemic attitude of *taking-to-be-true* (or *assent*). In contrast to knowledge, belief requires only subjectively sufficient reasons but lacks objectively sufficient reasons.[38] Can these interpretations, though not dealing directly with ideas, offer a plausible account of the regulative use of ideas?

In a recent proposal, Schafer (2023) develops a noumenalist reading of the supreme principle of reason (see 2.2). According to Schafer, Kant defends a version of the supreme principle that '*does* commit us to the bare existence of the "whole series of conditions" and so to the unconditioned', even though 'that commitment leaves the nature of the thing or things we are committed to almost wholly indeterminate' (Schafer 2023:175). Schafer construes this commitment as doctrinal belief or 'assent' that is 'necessary for theoretical reason to

---

[36] In the cited passage, Kant considers it a misunderstanding to characterize ideas as 'concepts of real things'. Such a characterization may be impossible for the cosmological ideas (see A673/B701). The term *noumenon* literally translates as the object of '*noûs*' (Greek for 'intellect' or 'reason'). This interpretation seems to imply the use of the term in the positive sense, meaning an 'intelligible object' (A256/B311) that is 'outside of our sensibility' (B307). Related notions include a 'thing of thought (an *ens rationis*)' (A337/B394) and a 'being of reason' (A681/B709). By contrast, the term used in the negative sense is a 'boundary concept' (A255/B311) or 'a concept setting limits to sensibility' (A256/B311). See 5.3.

[37] For example, Ameriks (2003), Chignell (2007b), Kreines (2009, 2017), Wuerth (2014), Pickering (2016), Watkins (2016, 2019b), Stang (2016), Proops (2021), Schafer (2023).

[38] In the Doctrine of Method (in the Canon of Pure Reason, A820ff./B848ff.), Kant distinguishes three kinds of taking-to-be-true (or assent): *knowing* requires both subjectively and objectively sufficient reasons, *believing* requires only subjectively sufficient reasons, and *opining* lacks both subjectively and objectively sufficient reasons. For discussion, see Chignell (2007a, 2007b) and Watkins and Willaschek (2020).

successfully engage in its essential activities' (Schafer 2023:173). So, Schafer allows for assent to the existence of something unconditioned but concedes that the content of what is assented to must remain 'almost wholly' indeterminate. In this way, Schafer's view can avoid the transcendental fallacies that arise from the determination of the unconditioned by our categories. Any determination would transform the regulative use into a constitutive use of reason. Can we take this view to develop an account of the regulative use of ideas?[39]

At first glance, the proposal offers a natural explanation for the legitimacy and the normative bindingness of ideas: their regulative use is legitimate and binding because it is backed by a commitment to the existence of something unconditioned. The unconditioned is assumed to ground (in some sense) what the ideas demand us to realize, that is, it grounds the systematic unity of cognitions that reason demands us to seek. But this proposal also raises some worries.

First, a worry regarding the *indeterminacy* of doctrinal belief. Ideas of reason are concepts that complete a particular 'whole series of condition' and contain specific predicates such as <simple substance> or <fundamental power>. If the regulative use of any idea involves the same commitment to the bare, but entirely indeterminate existence of something unconditioned, then the view cannot explain the differences between ideas. It appears that regardless of the kind of idea we use, in all cases we are committed only to the 'bare existence of the unconditioned in a highly abstract form' (Schafer 2023:174). This might be unsatisfactory as an account of ideas. If the commitment is entirely indeterminate, we may lack a sufficient justification for why we ought to use these ideas rather than others.

Second, a worry regarding a potential *objectification*. If we instead assume that each idea presupposes a different belief, then it might be difficult to defend the claim of the indeterminacy of these beliefs. The regulative use of the idea of the soul may presuppose a belief in the existence of thinking substances, while the idea of God may presuppose a belief in an author of a purposively ordered world. This suggests that the beliefs differ in content depending on the idea they ground. However, it might be difficult to spell out these differences in content without allowing a determinative use of the categories. We may run the risk of slipping from a regulative into a constitutive use and determine the unconditioned as an object for us according to our categories.[40] But then we do exactly what Kant warns against in the Dialectic: we 'hypostatize' ideas, that is, 'mak[e] thoughts into things' (A395; see also A384, B402, A615/B643), instead of

---

[39] I concede that the *doctrinal-belief* accounts are not explicitly aimed at explaining the regulative use of ideas. Regardless of my criticism in this subsection, they may offer plausible arguments for an existential commitment to the unconditioned at a different level of explanation.

[40] On the relative use of the categories regarding things-in-themselves, see also Adickes 1924:75–95.

regarding ideas as 'imagined object[s]' (A670/B698) or 'analogues of real things' (A674/B702). Indeed, the significance of ideas is 'misunderstood' if they are taken 'for concepts of real things' (A643/B671) or for things 'assumed in themselves' (A674/B702). Thus, if the regulative use of ideas requires doctrinal beliefs, these should not be understood as positing the existence of metaphysically robust objects that correspond exactly to these ideas, as this would lead to transcendental fallacies (see A327/B383, A643/B671).[41]

Third, there is a worry regarding the *subjectivity* of doctrinal beliefs. Doctrinal belief requires only subjectively sufficient reasons, which Schafer construes as 'sufficiency with regard to reason's purposes' (Schafer 2023:171). Drawing on doctrinal belief only explains why ideas are justified subjectively with regard to reason's own inferential procedures. But it does not explain why their regulative use gives rise to principles of systematic unity that have 'objective but indeterminate validity' (A663/B691), 'as pertaining to the object itself' (A650/B678). These principles are often characterized as 'transcendental' presuppositions. For example, we must presuppose that nature itself is systematically unified (e.g., A321/B378ff., A327/B383–384, A681/B709ff.). Conceding a mere belief may be too weak to justify the transcendental status of ideas. For a belief, while subjectively warranted, could still turn out to be objectively false. That is, the unconditioned that the belief postulates could after all not exist. Appealing to doctrinal belief might thus not be effective in justifying the objective validity of regulative ideas.[42]

1.6 Fictionalism: Ideas As Non-Referring Fictions

A fictionalist view implies that ideas provide empty or nonreferring fictions. Their legitimate use requires the rejection of any existential commitment to what these fictions describe. Fictionalism finds its most explicit support in passages that describe the regulative use of ideas in terms of 'heuristic' (rather than ostensive) principles (A663/B691, A671/B699) or 'heuristic fictions' (A771/B799). Such heuristic fictions are subjectively necessary guidelines to pursue the 'demands' (e.g., A656/B684, A699/B727) and 'interests' of reason

---

[41] There may be ways in which the account can escape this criticism. If doctrinal belief is understood as analogous to practical belief (see A825/B854), it may not involve the assent of a theoretical judgement about an unconditioned object. Such a practical belief is then a necessary presupposition for our cognitive activities, like a practical postulate for moral action (e.g., Schafer 2023:172–177, see also Willaschek 2018:272–274). This view might come close to the perspectivalist view defended in Sections 4 and 5.
[42] On this criticism, see also Kraus (2020:188–190). Stang (2016:282) proposes an additional criterion for rational belief in terms of intersubjective validity. This would still not eliminate the worry that the whole collective of rational subjects might be mistaken about the unconditioned.

(e.g., A666–678/B694–696, A686/B704, A704/B732) rather than truthful descriptions of a mind-independent reality.[43]

Fictionalism takes seriously that ideas should not simply be understood as 'concepts of real things' (A643/B671). By renouncing any relation that ideas might have to an underlying reality, it avoids sliding into a constitutive use of ideas that illegitimately determines non-sensible objects. Many commentators therefore consider the regulative use as a species of the logical use of reason. They identify the regulative use of reason with the application of the logical principle to seek systematic unity in cognition through logical inference. They grant that this subjective principle presupposes – in some sense – the transcendental principle that nature really *is* systematically unified.[44] Yet this transcendental principle is considered to be only a 'self-serving delusion' (Guyer 1979:42), an 'inevitable illusion' or 'illusory postulation of reason' (Grier 2001:263, 276). The regulative use is thus necessarily based on a natural and unavoidable transcendental illusion, that is, the 'transcendental and illusory postulation that nature ... is already given as a complete whole' (Grier 2001:275). Such use still involves the 'hypostatization' of the idea as the 'object of ... [scientific] knowledge' (Grier 2001:279), and hence as the 'intelligible ground' of *all* appearances in nature (Grier 2001:297, 301; see A384, A395, B402, A615/B643). Yet in order not to fall prey to this illusion and commit a metaphysical fallacy, it is assumed that this object, the referent of the idea, does not exist.

A major worry is that fictionalism fails to offer a suitable explanation for why ideas – employed as regulative principles – are normatively binding at all. The fictionalist is faced with the following situation: on the one hand, ideas facilitate, or even enable, the activities of the understanding in seeking systematic cognition of nature; on the other hand, ideas lead to illusory postulations that do not even have a referent. Yet the emptiness of ideas undermines the normative bindingness of the principle of systematicity. For how can an illusory assumption generate a prescriptive force for our epistemic activities that aim at the truth-apt cognition of empirical objects?[45]

---

[43] This line of interpretation was famously proposed by Vaihinger (1911) and can also be found in Cassirer (1999). For a classic critique, see Adickes (1927). In recent scholarship fictionalist interpretations are offered by Grier (2001), Guyer (2003), Allison (2004), Dyck (2014), McLaughlin (2014), and – with qualifications, as discussed at the end of this subsection – in Willaschek (2018:254–269).

[44] In the third *Critique*, the principle of systematicity is characterized as 'a subjectively necessary transcendental *presupposition*' (FI 20:209, see also CJ 5:181) and associated with the reflective power of judgement.

[45] Some proponents of fictionalism explicitly assign a prescriptive function to reason in that it prescribes ends to theoretical enquiries (Grier 2001:276; also Zuckert 2017). Yet grounding the prescriptive force of reason on empty or false theoretical claims seems problematic. For discussion, see Kraus (2020:190–193).

In reply to this worry, the regulative use of ideas is often modelled on *hypothesis formation* in science. Ideas are assumed to be primarily involved in higher-order scientific theorizing, specifically in the discovery and articulation of empirical laws of nature.[46] An idea's regulative use consists then in the assumption of a certain hypothesis about a non-sensible object (e.g., that an appearance must be grounded in the existence of an unconditioned subsistent thing). This hypothesis serves as the highest premise in an ascending series of empirical conditions, without, however, being asserted as true. This hypothesis-formation view can apparently construe the regulative use as a real use.[47] To avoid the transcendental illusions that may follow from a real use, the hypothesis is only accepted problematically in order to bring more 'unity into particular cognitions as far as possible' (A647/B675), without assuming a reference to something real.[48]

The hypothesis-formation view also raises both textual difficulties and philosophical worries. For Kant argues that the hypothetical use is possible only if it is itself 'directed' at the 'systematic unity of the understanding's cognitions' (A647/B675). The hypothetical use, therefore, presupposes the more basic 'indispensably necessary regulative use' of an idea, which first defines a systematic unity (A644/B672). Moreover, Kant explicitly denies that ideas can be used to form hypotheses, at least according to Kant's conception of a hypothesis, which requires the relation to what is 'actually given' in appearance (A770/B798). But ideas of reason precisely lack this relation to given appearances and therefore, if used in a 'transcendental hypothesis ... for the explanation of things in nature, would thus be no explanation at all' (A772/B800).[49] The hypothesis-formation view thus cannot offer a satisfying answer to the problem of normative bindingness either.

---

[46] See Grier (1997, 2001:288–292), also Willaschek (2018:168). For applications of the regulative use of reason in Kant's philosophy of science, see, for example, Buchdahl (1969, 1971), Kitcher (1986), Sturm (2009:127–182), Ginsborg (2017), Zuckert (2017), and Kraus (2023).

[47] Willaschek (2018, esp. 103–126) effectively criticizes the identification of the regulative use with the logical use of reason and allows for both a regulative use and a constitutive use of the supreme principle of reason. For Willaschek, only the regulative use of the supreme principle is legitimate and consists in the hypothetical assumption of its descriptive content. By contrast, its constitutive use, that is, the taking-to-be-true of its descriptive content, leads to an illegitimate transcendental illusion. Willaschek's distinction allows ideas to have a real use that can be either regulative or constitutive (Willaschek 2018:171, 186).

[48] It is questionable in what sense the regulative use of ideas can still be considered as a real use if they 'lack objective reality', as Willaschek (2018:254) contends. If the view remains agnostic regarding the reference to an existing reality, it faces a problem of subjectivity as the *doctrinal-belief* view, discussed in 1.5. On the objective reality of ideas, see Adickes 1924:75–95.

[49] On this point, see also Spagnesi (2023a:677) and 5.1.

Can we nonetheless understand the regulative function of ideas in analogy with *scientific idealizations*? Even if a scientific hypothesis is false or empty and therefore no longer a candidate for a law of nature, it might be an idealization that, while not strictly true, can be pragmatically useful as a scientific model. For example, Newton's laws of motion provide an adequate model for the motions of bodies at sufficiently low velocities in many contexts, although strictly speaking they are invalidated by Einstein's theory of relativity. The assumption of certain fundamental particles of matter can be a useful mathematical idealization, even though we do not (yet) have experiments that prove the existence of these particles. Similarly, ideas may fulfil the role of *idealizations* rather than true descriptions of an underlying reality. In this sense, ideas may define what Philip Kitcher calls the 'ideal limit of inquiry' (Kitcher 1986:214). For Kitcher, what counts as a causal law can be understood only against the background of a system that would result from an ideally extended inquiry. Ideas provide only the framing conditions for our minds to recognize general patterns and explain the observed real dependencies between different appearances.

This view, however, raises the question of how to evaluate the progress of our scientific inquiries to make sure we are approaching the ideal limit. If the ideal limit is defined only in terms of a system-internal standard, such as the increase in internal systematicity, then the view faces similar challenges as a coherence theory of truth: it cannot assess progress by objective criteria or in terms of a reality that exists independently of human minds as the ultimate target of human cognition. In other words, if one denies ideas any relation to a mind-independent reality, one may also have to give up on a mind-independent standard by which to measure the adequacy of our scientific endeavours. That is, by denying that ideas even indeterminately point us to the existence of something absolutely unconditioned that grounds our cognition, fictionalism may be forced to dispense with objective criteria of truth or even with a non-relativist account of truth altogether.[50]

These discussions of noumenalism and fictionalism suggest that an adequate interpretation of ideas of reason should preserve the true core of each view: the productive aspects of ideas as heuristic fictions of the human mind that promote the systematization of cognitions and the realist aspects of ideas that allow a relation to a mind-independent reality but refrain from postulating metaphysically robust objects of ideas.

---

[50] Kitcher (1986) assumes that Kant holds such a coherence (or pragmatist) theory of truth. This seems at odds with Kant's definition of truth as the 'agreement of cognition with its object' (A58/B82). See 2.2 and 5.2.

2 The Two Functions of Reason in Human Cognition

An interpretation of the regulative ideas of reason should explain their *transcendental* role with respect to the empirical cognition of nature, while avoiding two temptations:[51] to reintroduce descriptive claims about real things in a metaphysically robust sense, and to reduce these ideas to non-referring but pragmatically useful fictions. To understand the need for a transcendental role of reason, Subsection 2.1 shows why the understanding is fundamentally incomplete in its endeavour to produce empirical cognition: the understanding is subject to conceptual underdetermination and lacks sufficient criteria of truth. These shortcomings make it necessary for the understanding to seek guidance from reason in two respects: in assessing the truth of empirical cognition (2.2) and in forming empirical concepts (2.3).

2.1 The Incompleteness of the Understanding

Section 1 has shown that reason and the understanding are closely related. The understanding is an 'object for reason', as the senses are an object for the understanding (A664/B692). Reason does not relate directly to objects of experience, but to the concepts and cognitions of the understanding (e.g., A335/B392), or to the 'actions of the understanding' (e.g., A321/B378, A327/B383). But why does the understanding need a higher authority to direct it at all? There are two important aspects in which the understanding is incomplete: determining conceptual content and tracking truth.

The understanding is essentially the 'capacity to judge', and its central task is to make judgements with objective content, that is, theoretical cognitions (A81/B106). Such cognitions are judgements that are taken to be about an object and to have objective validity, that is, validity for everyone.[52] In order for a judgement to be about an empirical object, the object itself must be given (or at least able to be given) to the senses. The understanding thus relies on sensibility for an immediate representation of something particular in intuition. For example, the cognition that *this rose is red* requires me to have an empirical intuition of a spatio-temporal particular, such as my visual impression of the flower on my windowsill. This intuited particular is then reflected under the concept <rose> and specified by the predicate <red>.[53]

---

[51] The transcendental role of reason in experience is rarely acknowledged or sufficiently explained in the literature. Notable exceptions include Buchdahl (1967), O'Shea (1997), Abela (2006), Massimi (2017, 2021), Hoffer (2019, 2023), Geiger (2022), Spagnesi (2022, 2023a, 2023b).

[52] I set aside the question of whether *judgements of perception*, which are merely subjectively valid, count as judgements in the relevant sense (see P 4:304–305). For discussion, see Kraus (2020:21–22).

[53] For an excellent account of the two conditions of empirical cognition – givenness to sensibility and thinkability through concepts – see Watkins and Willaschek (2017). On spatio-temporal

Kant spills much ink in the first *Critique* explaining how the understanding and sensibility interact with one another such that they can produce empirical cognition. The Transcendental Analytic analyses how the understanding imprints its a priori forms on sensibility, which are then transcendental conditions of experience: the logical forms of judgement not only define how concepts can be unified in a judgement, but – employed as categories – they also provide rules for the sensible synthesis by which a manifold of intuition is unified (see A79/B104–105). Only if this sensible synthesis is carried out in accordance with these categories can it provide the appropriate kind of empirical matter for the cognition of an object of experience. The resulting cognition not only displays the logical forms, but also reflects real dependence relations in the object. For example, <The rose is red> not only displays the logical form of a categorical judgement <S is P>, but also, if appropriately related to intuition, reflects the dependence relation between a substance (e.g., the particular rose I see) and its accidents (e.g., redness). Far into the first *Critique*, it looks as if the understanding and sensibility together are quite capable of generating cognition with objective content. There is no significant mention of reason in this part of the book. Yet the understanding faces challenges of underdetermination, for which sensibility by itself cannot provide succour.

2.1.1 Conceptual Underdetermination

Empirical cognition results from reflecting intuitions under empirical concepts within a judgement. To form a judgement, one must have acquired a set of empirical concepts. The possession of an empirical concept presupposes an understanding of the conditions under which a concept is suitably formed and appropriately applied to an object. To make the judgement <The rose is red>, one has to understand what the concepts <rose> and <red> mean: namely what their empirical content (or intension) is and to which objects they can be meaningfully applied (i.e., their sphere or extension). It makes good sense to apply a colour concept to a spatial object with a surface, but it is not meaningful to judge that *the number 2 is green*, that *my joy has yellow dots*, or that *the principles of democracy are purple*. But where does the understanding get its concepts from? The understanding itself provides only pure concepts – the categories – which define the logical structure of experience, but which do not contain empirical content.

In his *Lectures of Logic*, Kant depicts a complex process of empirical concept acquisition: it involves the comparison of different sensible representations, their

---

particulars, see, e.g. Allais (2015:153–168). I do not consider non-empirical kinds of cognition, e.g., mathematical or philosophical cognition.

reflection in terms of common sensible marks, and the abstraction of these marks into an empirical concept.[54] The resulting empirical concept is defined by its content (i.e., the sensible marks) and its extension (i.e., the set of objects that can be aptly reflected under it). In the Appendix to the Dialectic, Kant adds another layer to his account, as he worries that there is some '*indeterminacy* of the logical sphere' (A656/B684). Now, assuming the senses provide concepts with empirical content in terms of sensible marks, it might be plausible for certain simple concepts, like <red>, to be extracted directly from sensible intuition (e.g., in terms of the sensible mark of redness). But this account does not seem plausible for more complex concepts. Even concepts such as <rose> and <tree> might not be simply read off of sensible intuition alone. Rather, their content seems to be meaningfully defined only in relation to other concepts such as <plant>, <leaves>, <stem>, <thorns>, <tulip>, <orchid>, and so forth, which defines their commonalities as well as their specific differences. Hence, concepts are defined in terms of their relations to both more general genus-concepts and more specific species-concepts.

It has been convincingly argued that Kant would fall back into a kind of direct realism (as a variant of empiricism) that would be alien to Kant's transcendental idealism, if he allowed sensible marks to be read directly off of intuitions.[55] Neither the understanding nor sensibility could answer the question whether the proximate genus under which <red> falls is <colour> or <photoreceptor stimulant>. The Appendix therefore suggests a view according to which the content of an empirical concept can be appropriately defined only within 'a certain systematic unity of all possible empirical concepts' (A652/B680). The principles of systematicity provided by reason, as we will see in Subsection 2.2, thus play a decisive role.

2.1.2 Tracking Real Dependence Relations

To gain deeper insights into the nature of an object, we use inferences to derive further properties or explanations for certain characteristics of objects. For such inferences to be possible, cognitions must stand in entailment relations to one another. These relations reflect the relations of the empirical concepts used in these cognitions. Once I have understood further distinguishing marks of

---

[54] For example, JL 9:94–95. For an excellent account, see Longuenesse (1998:107–130). A mark is the 'ground of cognition ... in the comparison of things' (Log-W 24:834) and, as such, it gives rise to predicates entailed *in* a concept (see JL 9:58ff., Log-Bl 24:106). I remain neutral on whether marks are merely *sensible* or in some sense *conceptual*. See also Ginsborg (2006) and Anderson (2014).

[55] On this argument, see Geiger (2003), Anderson (2014), and Kraus (2023). For an opposite view, see Ginsborg (2006).

<rose>, I can draw conclusions about the particular rose I cognize, such as that *the rose has a stem with thorns*, that *the flower is not a tulip*, and that *the rose thrives best when it has at least six full hours of sunlight a day*. But how can the understanding make sure that it is tracking the correct entailment relations, namely the real dependence relations between the objects (and their states) being judged? If the object I see has no thorns, have I misapplied the concept <rose> to the object of my current intuition? Or am I mistaken in assuming that the content of <rose> entails the marks of <having a stem with thorns>? In other words, are the cognitions I hold about the object true? Are the general laws of nature that explain the distinctive characteristics of roses true?

Whether our cognitions track real dependence relations in objects is a matter of *truth*. Scientific revolutions in history have shown that scientific concepts and laws and even the entities considered fundamental, which were long believed to be appropriate, had to be revised to better grasp the dependencies in objects. Just think of the revision of the laws of motion from Newton to Einstein, the redefinition of mass with the finding of Einstein's energy-mass equivalence, and the abandoning of phlogiston theory. But how can we decide whether a cognition, or a related set of cognitions, is in fact true or not?

Kant holds a correspondence theory according to which *truth* is nominally defined as the 'agreement [of cognition] with the object' (A820/B848).[56] Whether, for example, my cognition *that the rose is red* is true depends on whether the object that I thereby cognize is actually a red rose. A difficulty for Kant is that this agreement is hard to assess, since we have no access to the object 'outside' of representation. For we lack insight into the real grounds that make our cognition true, independently of our representational faculties. Therefore, we cannot evaluate truth absolutely with regard to a mind-independent reality, but only relatively in relation to how things appear to us.[57] But even if we only examine the *empirical truth*, that is the truth of an empirical cognition in light of an object given in intuition, we lack suitable criteria to decide whether a particular cognition actually corresponds to its object.[58]

Kant's correspondence theory of truth cannot give us a 'general and certain criterion' for assessing truth (A58/B82), 'a criterion ... that is certain, universal,

---

[56] See also A58/B82, A157/B197, A191/B236, A237/B296, A642/B670, JL 9:50.

[57] See: 'I can compare the object with my cognition, however, only *by cognizing it*. Hence my cognition is supposed to confirm itself, which is far short of being sufficient for truth' (JL 9:50); 'without [possible experience], every concept is ... without truth and reference to an object' (A489/B517). See Posy (1981).

[58] Kant frequently employs the notion of 'empirical truth' (A146/B185, A191/B236, A202/B248, A451/B479, A492/B520, A651/B679; JL 9:66), and occasionally contrasts it with 'transcendental truth' (A146/B185, A222/B269): the former concerns the agreement of an empirical cognition with an object of possible experience (see A58/B82, A157/B197, A191/B236, A642/B670); the latter concerns only 'the relation to the form of experience' (A222/B269).

and useful in application' (JL 9:50), or a 'touchstone (*Prüfstein*) of the correctness' of a set of cognitions (A65/B90). Sensibility by itself cannot prove truth with certainty, since it can only provide 'merely *subjective* grounds' and even lead us to 'confuse *the mere illusion of truth with truth itself*' (JL 9:54). Sensible intuitions are necessary to give us access to objects, provide evidence of their actuality, and contribute sensible matter to cognition. Yet they do not offer objective grounds or prove with certainty that objects really display certain characteristics or behaviors. Neither can the understanding with its formal principles of cognition nor reason in its logical use of inference provide any criteria of truth. However, reason's principle of systematicity can supply 'touchstones of truth' (A647/B675), as we will see in Subsection 2.3.

In sum, the understanding is incomplete in generating objective content in two respects: solely based on sensible marks, it cannot sufficiently determine the empirical content of the concepts it operates with, and it cannot find sufficient criteria of truth to assess whether its cognitions track real dependence relations. While the understanding can provide *necessary formal conditions* for the kind of content that can be predicated in general, it lacks *sufficient conditions* for empirical content, specifically for the semantic determination of *empirical* concepts and the truth-assessment of *empirical* cognitions. Before returning to ideas of reason, I argue in the remainder of this section that reason's general demand for systematic unity complements the semantic and the epistemic functions of the understanding. In the first part of the Appendix (A642/B670–A668/B696), Kant first provides an argument for reason's epistemic function in providing a 'sufficient mark of empirical truth' (A647/B675–A651/B679) and then a second argument for its semantic function in concept-formation (A651/B679–A664/B692). Let us look at these arguments in turn.

2.2 The Assessment of Empirical Truth

In the Appendix, reason's demand for systematic unity is understood to provide criteria of truth (see A647/B675–A651/B679). Kant elaborates on an argument that, starting from the logical principle of reason to seek systematic unity, shows the necessity of a 'transcendental principle of reason' concerning the systematic unity of nature itself (A648/B676). The central passage reads as follows:

> For the law of reason to seek unity is necessary, since without it we would have no reason, and without that, no coherent use of the understanding, and, lacking that, no sufficient mark of empirical truth; thus in regard to the latter we simply have to presuppose the systematic unity of nature as objectively valid and necessary. (A651/B679)

This passage implies that reason's demand for systematic unity is not only essential for reason, but also necessary for a 'coherent use of the understanding' and thus for obtaining a 'sufficient mark of empirical truth'. The argument can be reconstructed as a *reductio ad absurdum*:[59]

Premise 1: Assume for the sake of the argument that reason did not seek systematic unity.

Premise 2: If reason did not seek systematic unity, then there would be no reason (since the subjective law to seek unity is essential to reason).

Premise 3: If reason did not demand systematic unity from the understanding, then there would be no *coherent use of the understanding* (that is, cognitions could not be formed such that they stand in inferential relations to one another).

Premise 4: If there were no coherent use of the understanding, then it would not be possible to obtain a *sufficient mark of empirical truth*.

Premise 5: (*implicit*) If there were no sufficient mark of empirical truth, then it would not be possible to evaluate the truth of cognition (which would be an absurd conception of cognition).

Conclusion 1: Thus, the subjective *law of reason* to seek unity is *necessary* for truth-evaluable cognition.

Conclusion 2: Thus, the *transcendental principle* that nature is a systematic unity must be presupposed as objectively valid.

The remarkable result of this argument is that nature itself must be assumed to be systematic. The demand for systematic unity is not only a subjective principle, but a 'transcendental principle of reason' that must be assumed as objectively valid (A648/B676).

In an explicit application of this transcendental principle, reason serves as the arbiter of empirical truth: reason generates a working hypothesis to test whether particular cognitions are 'coherently connected' (A647/B675) in a chain of syllogistic reasoning. This is the hypothetical use of reason, which – as a special case of the regulative use – supplies so-called 'touchstones' of truth for assessing cognitions (A647/B675). The criterion of epistemic coherence, in the simplest sense, consists in logical consistency: a set of cognitions should not mutually contradict each other; a working hypothesis should not contradict any

---

[59] This reconstruction and the following paragraph are adapted from Kraus (2020:234).

other already accepted cognition in a relevant set.[60] In an advanced sense, it perhaps requires the derivability of cognitions from a fundamental law. A cognition that does not pass the coherence test within a set of already accepted cognitions has to be rejected as false or at least as rationally unfounded.[61]

Hence, in addition to his correspondence theory of truth, Kant advocates a coherence theory (or, perhaps better, a systematicity theory) of epistemic justification.[62] By guiding the understanding to the systematic unity of all its cognitions, reason provides a formal method for evaluating truth that can apply both to the cognitions of a single subject and to cognitions across different subjects. What remains open at this point, however, is why this method requires a 'transcendental presupposition' regarding the systematic unity of nature itself (A651/B679, A678/B706). In my critique of noumenalism in Subsection 1.5, I argued that this presupposition should be understood neither as a determinative judgement about nature as a whole nor as a determinative judgement about something unconditioned that grounds appearances, since this would involve a transcendental fallacy. Section 4 will show that the formal criterion of systematicity can only be successfully applied if an idea of reason provides a sketch or blueprint of the whole system within which the criterion is applicable.

2.3 The Determination of Empirical Content

Since the dependence relations we track in cognition are directly related to the empirical concepts we use, the demand for systematicity is relevant not only for truth-evaluation, but also for the formation of empirical concepts. To avoid discrepancies and incoherencies among our cognitions as much as possible and to advance towards a more systematic description of nature, the more basic conceptualizing activities should also be guided by this demand.

In the next few paragraphs, Kant develops a similar argument for the formation of empirical concepts (A651/B679–A664/B692). The logical principle to seek systematic relations among concepts is primarily a subjective interest of reason. Yet a corresponding transcendental principle must be presupposed with 'objective but indeterminate validity' (A663/B691), 'because without it no empirical concepts and hence no experience would be

---

[60] See Kant's two 'formal criteria of truth' in the *Jäsche-Logic*: '1. the principle of contradiction, 2. the principle of sufficient reason' (JL 9:52).
[61] Kant grants that some judgements are 'immediately certain, e.g., between two points there can be only one straight line' (A261/B316–317). For discussion, see Posy (1983) and Willaschek (2018:47–56).
[62] I set aside questions about knowledge, as an epistemic attitude of taking-to-be-true (or assent) towards cognition (see A820ff./B848ff.). For discussion, see Stevenson (2003), Chignell (2007b), Watkins and Willaschek (2020).

possible' (A654/B682). More specifically, Kant distinguishes three logical principles of systematicity: the principles of homogeneity, specification, and continuity.[63] The principle of homogeneity is defined as the principle 'of the *sameness of kind* in the manifold under higher genera' (A657/B685), guiding us in seeking, for every pair of concepts, a genus-concept with a larger 'domain' such that both concepts can be subsumed under it (A654/B682). The principle of specification is defined as the principle 'of the *variety* of what is same in kind under lower species' (A657/B685), guiding us in seeking for every given concept further sub-concepts (or species-concepts) that are richer in 'content ([i.e.,] determinacy)' (A654/B682). By assuming continuity between different concepts, according to the principle 'of the *affinity* of all concepts' (A657/B685), we arrive at an interconnected hierarchical system that proceeds, not only vertically from elementary genus-concepts to fine-grained species-concepts, but also horizontally between neighbouring concepts.[64]

As with the argument about truth-criteria above (2.2), this argument aims to show that these logical principles each presuppose a corresponding 'transcendental principle' (A650/B678, A663/B691). These transcendental principles guarantee a priori that if the formation of each new concept (e.g., <tree>) is guided by the logical principles, then the conceptual containment relations between all empirical concepts (e.g., <plant>, <leaves>, <stem>, <roots>, <tulip>, <orchid>, etc.) can constitute an inferential system.

Whether these conceptual containment relations, however, adequately correspond to the real dependence relations between the appearances described by these concepts can be assessed only a posteriori in light of ongoing experience. This assessment requires criteria of truth, as discussed. Moreover, whether our empirical concepts will eventually lead to a complete system of cognitions also remains an open question.[65] The acquisition of empirical concepts must be understood as an ongoing complex activity of systematization according to the principles of generalization, specification, and continuity. In light of ongoing experience, our system of empirical concepts is continuously assessed and refined as to its adequacy by adding (or revising) increasingly comprehensive genus-concepts, increasingly determinate species-concepts, and further intermediary concepts. In

---

[63] See A652/B680–A658/B686; CJ 5:185–186; JL 9:96–97; also Log-Bl 24:240–260; Log-W 24:905–913; Log-D 24:755.

[64] For a detailed discussion of Kant's logic lectures, see Watkins (2013). This and the next paragraph are adapted from Kraus (2020:232–234).

[65] 'Now whether this completeness is sensibly possible is still a problem. Yet the idea of this completeness still lies in reason, irrespective of the possibility or impossibility of connecting empirical concepts to it adequately' (A417/B444).

turn, newly acquired concepts inform the ongoing activity of acquiring empirical cognition, which aims at a system of cognitions.[66]

What, again, remains open at this point is the transcendental status of these three principles. As with the principle of systematicity in truth-evaluation, the principles of homogeneity, specification, and continuity are by themselves *topic-neutral*: Like the pure categories of the understanding, they can be applied to any subject matter. But in their topic-neutral form, I contend, they cannot provide the kind of guidance and direction that the understanding seeks to obtain from reason. Reason must offer more: it must outline domains in which these formal principles can take a foothold in reality and become applicable to a particular subject matter. This, I will argue in Section 4, is the regulative use of its ideas.

3 Kant's Visual Metaphors: *Standpoint, Horizon,* and *Focus Imaginarius*

In the Appendix to the Dialectic, Kant illustrates the regulative role of reason with a set of visual metaphors such as *standpoint, field of view, horizon,* and *focus imaginarius*. Reason, for example, 'prepares the field for the understanding' (A657/B685), 'posits an idea ... as a unique standpoint' (A681/B709), captures the 'universal and true horizon' of human insight (A659/B687), and directs the understanding to a '*focus imaginarius*' (A644/B672). A brief analysis of these metaphors will motivate the perspectivalist interpretation that I am going to develop in Sections 4 and 5. This section examines the use of these metaphors in the *Critique of Pure Reason* and in selected *Lectures on Logic*: Subsection 3.1 focusses on the notions of a *standpoint* and a *horizon*, whereas Subsection 3.2 discusses the metaphor of a *focus imaginarius*.[67]

3.1 The *Standpoint* and *Horizon* of Human Experience

The visual metaphors of *standpoint* and *horizon* were a common theme in eighteenth-century German philosophy. Gottfried W. Leibniz and Georg F. Meier, for example, use them to explore epistemological questions about the scope of human knowledge, often in comparison with divine knowledge.[68]

---

[66] Anderson (2014:369–372) offers a compelling account of concept-formation in terms of a 'qualified form of holism about conceptual content' (Anderson 2014:364). He distinguishes the logical aspects of a system from the irreducibly synthetic aspects of conceptual content, while acknowledging their mutual interdependence. See also Geiger (2003).

[67] In her perspectivalist interpretation, Massimi (2021:3279) helpfully distinguishes between two types of 'perspectival knowledge': 'knowledge *from* a vantage point' and 'knowledge *towards* a vantage point'. This distinction captures the bidirectional nature indicated in Kant's metaphors: there is a *standpoint* from which we acquire knowledge and a *focus imaginarius* towards which our knowledge is directed.

[68] For example, Leibniz (1693), Baumgarten (1750/1758), and Meier (1752). On the metaphor of a *horizon* in modern philosophy, see Ritter et al. (1974, 3:1194–1200).

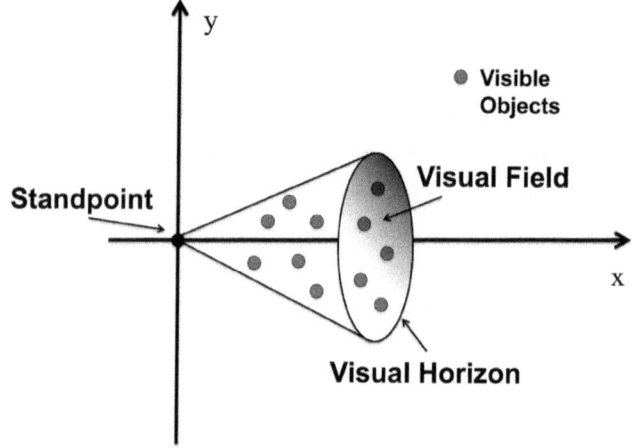

Figure 1 Schematic representation of the standpoint, the horizon, and the visual field of an observer.

In their literal meaning, these metaphors describe aspects of human vision. A standpoint is the specific spatio-temporal location, or vantage point, from which a spectator observes an object or scene. From this vantage point, the viewer can observe a certain 'field of view (*Gesichtsfeld*)' (or visual field) (A658/B686). Only objects within this visual field can be observed from that vantage point. Objects outside of it are not visible for the observer. If one moves to a different standpoint, the visual field changes accordingly: further phenomena may become available, while others may disappear. The 'horizon' denotes, strictly speaking, the border line of the visual field: the line that demarcates what can be seen from a certain standpoint from that which cannot be seen from it.[69] If you imagine yourself standing by the shores of the sea or on the top of a mountain, then the horizon is the line between the sea and the sky or, respectively, between the landscape and the sky. It is usually blurry, vague, and hard to discern. Figure 1 shows schematically the standpoint, the visual field, and the horizon of an observer.

Kant himself often characterizes his transcendental philosophy as the study of the 'human standpoint' (e.g., A26/B42), distinguishing himself from Leibniz's focus on divine knowledge.[70] For Kant, a main characteristic of the human standpoint is its *spatiotemporality*. All human subjects are located in space and time and have a distinctive spatiotemporal standpoint from which they intuit objects. While human beings differ in their distinctive

---

[69] The term *horizon* derives from Greek astronomy, meaning 'to divide', 'to delimit', or 'to demarcate', see Ritter et al. (1974, 3:1187–1190).
[70] See, e.g., Longuenesse (2005).

spatio-temporal standpoints, none of them can ever escape the limitations of space and time.[71] Despite their individual differences, they share a common 'human standpoint' from which they collectively explore the world and aim to accomplish an objective (or at least intersubjectively valid) description of nature.

In the Appendix, Kant uses the metaphors of *standpoint* and *horizon* specifically to illustrate the three general principles of concept-formation – the principles of homogeneity, specification, and continuity (see 2.3). He now considers a 'concept ... as a standpoint' and analyses the 'logical horizon' that it opens up (A658/B686). In general, a horizon is 'a multiplicity of things that can be represented and surveyed, as it were, from [the concept]' (A658/B686). This prima facie suggests a real definition of horizon: the *real horizon* of a concept is its extension, 'sphere' (e.g., A576/B604, A655/B683) or 'domain' (e.g., A71/B96, A654/B682). This is the set of objects that fall under the concept or that can be adequately reflected under it. For example, the real horizon of the concept <flower> is the set of items that can be correctly described as flowers. Kant uses the notion of a horizon vaguely here, so as to include the entire domain of things, rather than only the 'circle line' demarcating such a domain.[72]

But, in the Appendix, Kant specifies the *logical horizon* as follows:

> Within this horizon [of a concept] a multiplicity of points must be able to be given to infinity, each of which in turn has its narrower field of view; i.e., every species contains subspecies in accordance with the principle of specification, and the logical horizon consists only of smaller horizons (subspecies), but not of points that have no domain (individuals). (A658/B686)

A logical horizon does not contain things under it (i.e., individuals objects), but *sub-horizons*: these are the logical horizons of *subspecies*, that is, more specific concepts with smaller domains but more content. The principle of specification requires that each logical horizon encompasses further smaller horizons, but no complete individual concepts that fully determine an individual.[73]

In turn, the principle of homogeneity requires that each logical horizon can be enveloped in a further, more general horizon, the horizon of a higher genus-concept, until one reaches the highest genus and hence the 'universal and true horizon':

---

[71] Zuckert (2017, 2020) emphasizes that the transcendental illusions of reason can be understood as attempts to exit the human perspective.

[72] See also: 'That circle within which we can see things is called our horizon. The complex of things that man can cognize in a learned fashion ... is the horizon of his learned cognition' (Log-Bl 24:67), 'horizon, the circle that limits all objects' (Log-D 24:771). See also Meier's (1752) definition of the horizon as a 'sum total (*Inbegriff*)'.

[73] On the impossibility for humans to possess a lowest species-concept (*infima species*), see, e.g., A655/B683, JL 9:97, and Watkins (2013).

> But different horizons, i.e., genera, ... one can think as drawn out into a common horizon, which one can survey collectively from its middle point, which is the higher genus, until finally the highest genus is the *universal and true horizon*, determined from the standpoint of the highest concept and comprehending all manifoldness, as genera, species, and subspecies, under itself. (A658/B686–A659/B687, emphasis added)

With the metaphor of a logical horizon, Kant explores a new way of illustrating the relation of concepts to one another: genus-concepts and species-concepts are now understood as relating to one another as more or less encompassing horizons. The extent of the horizon's domain and the richness of its content are inversely proportional to each other: the larger the horizon of a concept, the poorer the concept's content but the larger its domain. The smaller the horizon of a concept, the richer its content but the smaller its domain.

For instance, the concept <plant> has a smaller, more specific horizon than the genus-concept <living being> and is therefore contained within the latter's horizon. But it has a larger, more general horizon than the species-concepts <rose>, <tulip>, and <orchid>. Its logical horizon encompasses the smaller horizons of the species-concepts <rose>, <tulip>, and <orchid>, but it is itself encompassed within the still wider logical horizon of the genus-concept <living being>. Figure 2 illustrates these examples. Searching for a more general genus-concept can now be understood in analogy with climbing up a mountain to enlarge one's visual field: in climbing up to a higher vantage point, one's visual field grows through merging multiple, more limited visual fields of lower vantage points at the foot of the mountain or in the valley.

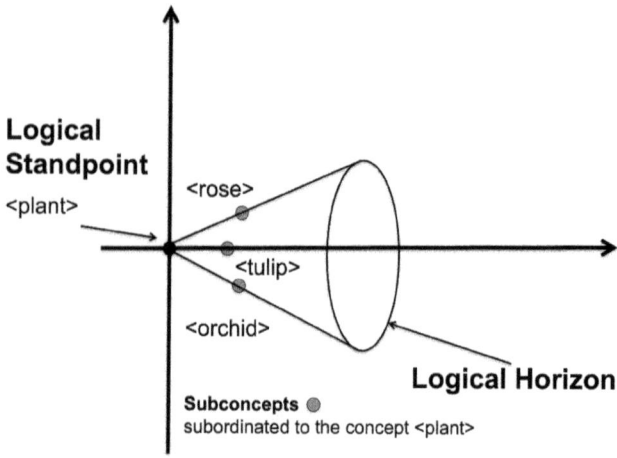

Figure 2 Schematic representation of the metaphorical notions of a logical standpoint and a logical horizon for the example of the concept <plant>.

Kant applies this analogy to illustrate the function of ideas of reason: the law of homogeneity leads us to the 'highest standpoint' of the most general genus-concept (A659/B687). This highest concept spans the 'universal and true horizon', which contains all other, more specific horizons (A659/B687). It thus defines the entire domain of human cognition, and this is precisely the function of ideas of reason, or so I will argue in Section 4.

The task of transcendental philosophy is, for Kant, to explore the boundaries of human understanding.[74] In the *Jäsche-Logic*, Kant describes this task as the 'determination of the horizon' of human cognition (JL 9:40). This task requires us to assess *'the congruence [Angemessenheit] of the quantity [Größe] of all cognitions with the capabilities [Fähigkeiten] and ends [Zwecke] of the subject'* (JL 9:40).[75] The horizon of human cognition is thus defined in relation to human capabilities: it concerns the adequacy relation between the domain of human cognition, on the one hand, and the faculties (and ends) of the human mind, on the other. The domain within which we can gain cognition at all must be adequate to our mental faculties. The Dialectic teaches us what errors we fall into if we ignore the limits of our cognition set by our capacities. The horizon of all human cognition thus characterizes the boundaries of human *'comprehensibility'* (Log-Bl 24:120) or *intelligibility*, as I will call it. But how can we possibly know our own horizon of understanding?

It seems that we are always caught in limited subjective horizons. The historical horizon of our time is constrained by historically contingent facts, such as language, culture, and the state of the art of the empirical sciences in a historical period (see JL 9:41). Moreover, each and every one of us has a *'private horizon'*: a horizon that 'depends upon various empirical conditions and special considerations, e.g., age, sex, station, mode of life, etc.' (JL 9:41). Philosophy, by contrast, should aim to explore the rational and universal horizon. A rational horizon is conditioned solely by the a priori insights gained through human reason that are universally valid for everyone, at all times and places (see JL 9:41). The 'absolute and universal horizon' is 'the congruence (*Congruenz*) of the limits of human cognitions with the limits of the whole of human perfection in general' (JL 9:41).

Now, we can understand Kant's theory of reason as offering some guidance for exploring the 'absolute and universal horizon' of the human standpoint in

---

[74] See, e.g., Axii, Bxx, Bxxiv, A11/B25, B128, B148, A154/B193, P 4:351–354.
[75] See also: 'The horizon is the congruence of the limits of our cognition with the ends of mankind' (Log-W 24:814); 'The horizon ... is the congruence <agreement> of the limits of any cognition whatever with the limits of human perfection' (Log-D 24:771).

general. In the Doctrine of Method, Kant illustrates reason's task in determining the human horizon as follows:

> Our reason [...] must [...] be compared with a sphere, the radius of which can be found out from the curvature of an arc on its surface (from the nature of synthetic a priori propositions), from which its content and its boundary can also be ascertained with certainty. Outside this sphere (field of experience) nothing is an object for it; indeed even questions about such supposed objects concern only subjective principles of a thoroughgoing determination of the relations that can obtain among the concepts of understanding inside of this sphere. (A762/B790)

Here Kant appeals to the metaphor of a horizon, too: reason defines 'the curvature of an arc on [the] surface' of a 'sphere', and this sphere is identified with the 'field of experience'. Reason's task is precisely to 'ascertain[] with certainty' the boundaries of this field, within which we can make out objects and 'outside [of which] ... nothing is an object for [human reason]'.

From this discussion, the following account emerges: human understanding is in principle limited by the universal horizon of the human standpoint. This horizon demarcates the domain within which humans can have cognition at all. It must primarily be adequate to our mental faculties and their distinctive forms (or formal conditions). The task of transcendental philosophy, and in particular of a critique of human reason, is to examine the a priori boundaries of this domain. These boundaries are a priori because they are not due to a mind-independent reality, but exclusively due to the limitations of our mental faculties themselves. The perspectivalist interpretation, as developed in Section 4, will suggest that ideas of reason serve as the highest genus-concepts opening up the *universal horizon of human understanding*.

3.2 The *Focus Imaginarius* and the World without Perspective

In the Appendix to the Dialectic, Kant borrows a further metaphor from optics: the *focus imaginarius* (A644/B672).[76] Kant has already introduced this metaphor in the *Dreams of a Spirit-Seer Elucidated by Dreams of Metaphysics* (1766) in order to dismantle the false pretensions of certain metaphysicians. There, he describes the visual metaphor as follows:

> Hence, if one takes the lines, which indicate the direction in which the light-rays enter the eye, and extend them backwards, the point at which they intersect is seen as a radiant point. ... In respect to the representation entertained, however, it is the *point of convergence* of the lines indicating the direction in

---

[76] Newton's *Opticks* (Axiom VIII) is often assumed to be the source of this metaphor. See Grier (2001, ch. 8) and Massimi (2021, sec. 3).

which the sensation is transmitted when it makes an impression (*focus imaginarius*). It is in this way that the place of a visual object, even when it is seen by one eye only, is determined. This happens, in particular, when the reflection of a body in a concave mirror is seen .... (DSS 2:344)

In the case of a visual reflection in a concave mirror, the *focus imaginarius* is the imaginary focal point that we assume behind the surface of the mirror and from which the mirror image seemingly proceeds. Looking at the mirror gives us the illusion that an object is located at this focal point. Yet whatever is represented to exist at the point is only a 'figment of my imagination' (DSS 2:245). If one assumes that there really is an object behind the mirror, then one falls prey to this optical illusion. In the *Dreams*, Kant uses this metaphor to illustrate his criticism of spirit-seers or dreamers of reason: even when fully awake, they 'transpose the illusion of their imagination and locate it outside themselves' and assume it to be an existing external thing 'in relation to their body' (DSS 2:343–344). Figure 3 shows the schematic account of Kant's metaphor of the *focus imaginarius*.

In the Appendix to the Dialectic, Kant uses the same metaphor to describe the use of ideas of reason. The regulative use of an idea consists in directing the understanding to a goal. This goal is, however, only a *focus imaginarius*, an imaginary focal point 'from which the concepts of the understanding do not really proceed' (A644/B672). We assume this point as the real ground from which our representations of reality seemingly proceed, 'as if these lines of direction were shot out from an object lying outside the field of possible empirical cognition (just as objects are seen behind the surface of a mirror)'

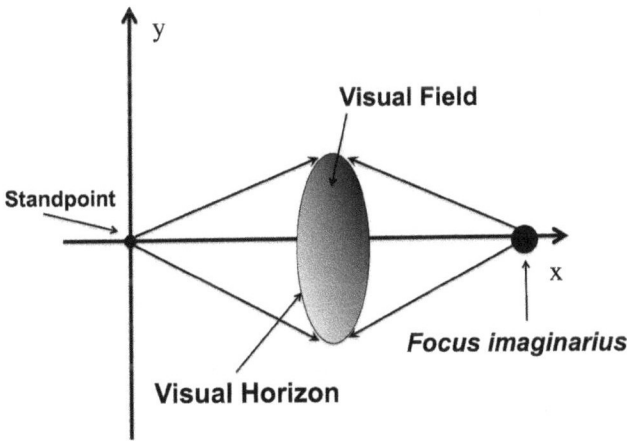

Figure 3 Schematic representation of Kant's visual metaphors of standpoint, visual field, horizon, and *focus imaginarius*.

(A644/B672). Unlike the horizon, the *focus imaginarius* is assumed to lie outside of the field of possible experience. Like the visual illusions in the case of the mirror image, the *focus imaginarius* leads to transcendental illusions that arise from our ideas of reason as 'natural' and 'unavoidable' (A298/B354, A422/B449–450, A462/B490).[77] But such an imaginary focal point is also 'indispensably necessary', since it 'serves to obtain ... the greatest unity alongside the greatest extension' of the understanding (A644/B672) and 'to take the measure of its greatest possible and uttermost extension' (A645/B673).

The metaphor of the *focus imaginarius* indicates a second function of ideas: ideas also project a goal for the understanding *beyond* the universal human horizon. From our finite perspective, it must remain imaginary, and that is precisely why it leads to transcendental illusions. Nonetheless, I will argue, in Section 5, that ideas – by projecting the *world without perspective* as a *focus imaginarius* – define normative ideals that are indispensable for our intelligibility of nature through cognition.

4 The Perspectivalist Interpretation: The Horizon of Human Experience

The final two sections offer a perspectivalist interpretation of the regulative use of reason. In Section 2, we learned that the understanding is fundamentally incomplete in its attempt to produce empirical cognitions with objective content: first, regarding the truth-assessment of empirical cognition and, second, regarding the formation of empirical concepts. As such, reason plays a transcendental role for the empirical cognition of nature. It complements the cognitive activities of the understanding in two ways: reason's demand for systematic unity provides criteria for the assessment of empirical truth (2.2) and reason's principles of homogeneity, specification, and continuity guide the determination of the empirical content of concepts within a system (2.3).[78]

The perspectivalist interpretation explains the specific role that transcendental ideas of reason have in complementing the understanding, while avoiding the two temptations diagnosed in Section 1: to reintroduce descriptive claims about real things in a metaphysically robust sense (1.5), and to reduce these ideas to non-referring but pragmatically useful fictions (1.6). The starting point is the insight that reason's general principles of systematicity are primarily formal and topic-neutral. To provide genuine orientation and guidance to the

---

[77] The naturalness and unavoidability of transcendental illusions play a central role in fictionalist interpretations, such as Grier (2001), Allison (2004), and Dyck (2014).

[78] The question of the transcendental status and objective validity of these principles, which remained open in Section 3, will be clarified in Section 5, as will the transcendental status and objective validity of ideas of reason.

understanding, reason must, however, delineate the domains of reality in which these formal principles can be meaningfully applied and gain a foothold in reality. The regulative function of ideas of reason is, then, to provide a sketch or blueprint of the whole system within which these principles are applicable.

The perspectivalist view centres on the following point: through the regulative use of transcendental ideas, reason supplies the contexts within which the understanding can properly operate and generate objective, truth-assessable content. These are the contexts within which empirical cognition can at all be meaningful from the human perspective in two respects. In a first dimension of meaning, the regulative use of ideas outlines what I call a *context of intelligibility*. This is a domain of reality in relation to which human experience has sufficiently conceptually determined content and amounts to inferentially related cognition of objects, that is, cognition that allows for inferences. In a second dimension of meaning, ideas are used to project what I call the ultimate *circumstances of evaluation* for empirical cognitions. This projection enables the derivation of normative standards for assessing empirical truth such that we can have objective grounds for assent.[79]

This section shows how the regulative use of ideas in the first dimension of meaning can be understood to generate contexts of intelligibility, which constitute the *universal horizons of the human standpoint*. Subsection 4.1 explains how an idea of reason relates to the empirical use of the understanding by defining a totality or maximal unity as the goal to be pursued by the understanding. Subsection 4.2 specifies how the idea provides rules for the cognitive activities of the understanding within this totality. Subsection 4.3 explicates this totality as the context of intelligibility within which the understanding can produce sufficiently determined and inferentially connected cognition. Subsection 4.4 shows how the proposed account applies to the idea of the soul and the idea(s) of the world-whole. These ideas define domains of nature

---

[79] A crucial clue to this interpretation came from a remark by Spohn (2016) about a possible interpretation of Kant according to a model of two-dimensional semantics, distinguishing two dimensions of meaning. In a first dimension, the semantic content of a sentence depends on the context of use, i.e., the totality of observable states of affairs. In a second dimension, the epistemic meaning or the cognitive significance of an expression that is used to express a belief depends on the possible world in which the belief is evaluated. Spohn (2016:1357) suggests that these two notions of contexts (or worlds) could map with qualifications on Kant's conceptions of the phenomenal and the noumenal world.

Posy (1981, 1983) also applies a language-theoretical model to Kant's transcendental idealism that distinguishes two components of the meaning of a judgement. What Posy calls 'truth-conditions', which 'describe what must be the case in the world at large for the judgment to be true' (Posy 1983:83) correspond to the truth-evaluative dimension in my view. What Posy calls 'assertability conditions', which 'set out the epistemic circumstances under which a properly constituted speaker may assert the judgment' comes close to the dimension of intelligibility in my view.

(i.e., of appearances) and the corresponding natural kinds to be found in these domains.

Section 5 will turn to the second dimension of meaning and highlight the role that ideas play for the normative assessment of empirical truth: by projecting ultimate circumstances of evaluation as imaginary focal points of human inquiry, reason sets domain-specific normative standards to assess the truth of empirical cognitions in this domain. These circumstances of evaluation can be identified with a *non-perspectival*, mind-independent reality, even though it must remain only imaginary for finite beings.

4.1 Guiding the Empirical Use of the Understanding

The perspectivalist interpretation offers an account of the distinctive role of the ideas of reason in complementing the cognitive activities of the understanding. How exactly does reason guide the understanding by means of its ideas? Recall that ideas of reason result from an iterative procedure, whereby reason seeks the totality of conditions. It does this in accordance with a particular form of inference that corresponds to a dependence relation, such as substantiality, causality, or interdependence. An idea is then the concept of an absolute whole that would complete the whole series of conditions or bring the series to a stop (see 2.3). It is also characterized as the 'concept of a maximum' (A327/B384) that cannot itself be given in experience and, more precisely, as the 'idea of the maximum of division and unification of the understanding's cognition' (A665/B693).[80] But why is such a maximum needed to advance the empirical use of the understanding? Why should it not suffice to apply the general principles of systematicity locally, find local systematic connections in small areas of empirical reality, and expand these local systematizations step by step? Why do we need an idea of a totality to direct the understanding to 'the greatest unity alongside the greatest extension' of its concepts and cognitions (A644/B672)?[81]

First, I argue that an idea outlines the maximal field of reality that we can hope to conceptualize and cognize in a systematic way at all. More specifically, *a transcendental idea defines a totality, or maximum, that reason prescribes to the understanding as an aim of perfection for its empirical use*. As such, the idea provides an a priori sketch or map of the context, as I will call it, in which the understanding can 'be brought into thoroughgoing agreement with itself' (A665/B693–A666/B694).

---

[80] On ideas as concepts of a maximum, see also A432/B460, A508/B536.
[81] Whether an idea represents a totality of conditions or something unconditioned (i.e., an absolute whole) depends on whether it serves to outline a context of intelligibility (4.3) or to project ultimate circumstances of evaluation (5.3).

To begin, we must note a fundamental difference from the categories of the understanding. Like the categories, the pure concepts of reason have an a priori origin (in this case, in the faculty of reason) and a transcendental status with respect to empirical cognition. They are therefore called *transcendental ideas*. But their transcendental status differs from that of the categories in that ideas relate *not* only to a single act of cognition, but 'to the entire use of the understanding' (A327/B384).

Before introducing the specific ideas of the soul, the world-whole, and God in the Transcendental Dialectic, Kant describes their general function as follows:

> [T]*ranscendental ideas* ... will determine the use of the understanding according to principles in the whole of an entire experience. (A321/B378)
>
> Thus reason relates itself only to the use of the understanding, ... in order to prescribe the direction toward a certain unity of which the understanding has no concept, proceeding to comprehend all the actions of the understanding in respect of every object into an *absolute whole*. (A326–327/B383)

Ideas thus relate not to single tokens of cognition or particular uses of the understanding, but rather 'to the *entire* use of the understanding' (A327/B384), 'the use ... in the *whole* of an *entire* experience' (A321/B378), or '*all* the actions of the understanding in respect of *every* object' (A326–327/B383, emphasis added). Ideas are not strictly necessary for a single use of the understanding, but they regulate the entire range of uses, including all past and future ones.

This difference can also be understood in terms of the distinction between *constitutive* and *regulative* use (see 1.4). The categories have a *constitutive* use regarding experience: they define strictly necessary conditions that must be instantiated in every single act of empirical cognition; otherwise, the resulting representation would not count as an instance of cognition. By contrast, transcendental ideas are '*never of constitutive use*, ... however, they have an excellent and *indispensably necessary regulative use*, namely that of directing the understanding to a certain goal' (A644/B672, emphasis added). A regulative use defines conditions or goals to be aspired towards in all possible uses of the understanding.

Ideas as concepts of a maximum or absolute whole are needed to 'prescribe the direction' and a goal to the understanding (A326/B383). Reason directs the understanding to areas of the world in search of further objects of cognition, further conditions of an object, and eventually empirical laws of nature. But it is unclear why ideas can prescribe goals to the understanding at all.

Somewhat confusingly, Kant sometimes presents the relation between ideas and the understanding as one of determination: ideas 'determine the use of the understanding according to principles' (A321/B378) or ideas '*consider* all experiential cognition *as determined* through an absolute totality of conditions' (A327/B384, emphasis added). But this kind of determination should not be understood in a constitutive sense as the determination of nature as a real thing. (This is the mistake of some versions of noumenalism, as discussed in 1.5). Rather, the phrase 'considering ... as determined' indicates the hypothetical nature of this determination.[82] At the level of cognitions, ideas define an absolute totality of conditions in which, if the totality existed, all cognitions would be fully determined.

This hypothetical formulation has led some commentators to construe the regulative use of ideas as the formation of hypotheses without asserting them. The cognizer, thus, remains neutral regarding their truth.[83] Despite this epistemic neutrality, these hypotheses must be assumed to derive cognitions and principles that can be taken to be true with regard to empirical objects. The regulative use of the idea of the soul would, for instance, include the hypothetical assumption that *I am a simple substance* and that *I have a fundamental mental power*. From these hypotheses, we can derive, according to this hypothesis-formation view, psychological laws and empirical cognitions of ourselves: for example, we can derive the cognition of a character trait from a temporal series of mental states, or infer a general law about human behaviour. Since we lack a corresponding intuition, the hypotheses based on ideas cannot be descriptions of empirical objects, but only of non-sensible objects.[84] Now, it is unclear how cognitions about me as an empirical person with diverse mental capacities, contingent behavioural patterns, and temporally distributed mental states could ever be derived from, or inferentially connected to, the a priori hypotheses that *I am a simple substance* and that *I have a fundamental mental power*. After all, as an empirical person I am never a simple substance and my empirical character always falls short of a complete systematic description. Moreover, as far as we know, there can be no simple soul-substances with a single fundamental power in nature. It is hard to see how idea-based hypotheses could serve as the most general description of the psychological beings we encounter empirically.[85]

---

[82] A hypothetical account is suggested by the hypothetical formulations of the principles derived from transcendental ideas. For example, following the idea of the soul, we 'connect all appearances ... of our mind ... *as if* the mind were a simple substance' (A672/B700).
[83] For example, Grier (2001) and Willaschek (2018). See 1.6.
[84] In 1.5, I used the terms 'noumenon', 'being[] of understanding', or 'being of reason' (see B306).
[85] See Spagnesi (2023a) and my critique in 1.6.

Thus, ideas do *not* direct the understanding by providing the most general descriptions of empirical reality as non-assertible hypotheses. An idea in principle does not function like the determining concepts of the understanding or, as Kant puts it, an idea is not 'the concept of an object' in the proper sense (A645/B673). Rather, reason operates on a meta-level: its ideas define the conditions under which the understanding can approach a completion and perfection of its empirical use, even though this completion and perfection can never be reached in experience itself. Ideas are 'concepts ... of the thoroughgoing unity of [the] concepts' of the understanding (A645/B673).[86] I take this to mean that ideas define an entire system of concepts that the understanding is demanded to fill in with appropriate empirical concepts.

Following his metaphor of the logical standpoint, Kant describes the regulative use as 'posit[ing] an idea only as a unique standpoint from which alone one can extend the unity that is so *essential* to reason and so *salutary* to the understanding' (A682/B710, emphasis added).[87] As a logical standpoint, an idea defines a systematic unity as the maximal extension of a system (of concepts or cognitions). This systematic unity is 'salutary' to the understanding because it prescribes how the understanding can come to perfection and completion. It prescribes the 'aim of a perfect systematic unity in our cognition'(A675/B703; also A681/B709) and thus enables the understanding to strive for 'a certain possible perfection of the cognition of [the] object' (A666/B694).[88] By orienting itself towards this aim, the understanding can approach 'the greatest unity alongside the greatest extension' of its cognitions (A644/B672) and 'the greatest possible unity of experience' (A678/B706). These notions of perfection and completion are indicated in the frequent use of superlatives in these and other passages:

> reason ... seeks to bring the greatest manifold of cognition of the understanding to the smallest number of principles (A305/B361);

> the greatest possible empirical use of my reason is grounded on an idea (that of systematic complete unity ...), which ... is unavoidably necessary for approximating to the highest possible degree of empirical unity (A677/B705).

Hence, transcendental ideas direct the understanding by defining a maximum towards which the understanding 'ought to proceed' (A685/B713), but of which it itself cannot have a concept. Prescribing a maxim is necessary for the

---

[86] See also: '[Reason] reserves for itself only the absolute totality in the use of concepts'(A326/B383). This does not preclude that we can posit an '*object in the idea*' (A670/B698); see 5.3.
[87] On concepts as standpoints with a logical horizon, see 3.1.
[88] This is in line with the Platonic conception of ideas as that which 'bring the legislative constitution of human beings ever nearer to a possible greatest perfection' (A317/B374). See 5.2.

understanding to come into a 'thoroughgoing agreement with itself' (A665/B693–A666/B694) and approximate a 'systematically coherent use of experience' (A786/B814, also A651/B679). It is precisely this normative dimension of reason as a meta-faculty of cognition that the hypothesis-formation view sketched above cannot capture. On the perspectivalist view, a full justification of this normativity is, however, only provided by the second role of ideas in projecting normative ideals (see 5.3).

Now, the maximum an idea prescribes cannot be given determinately. It is necessarily indeterminate and unattainable from the standpoint of experience.[89] The understanding can venture ever further in the direction of the goal without ever reaching it. It is radically open which empirical objects the understanding finds, which empirical concepts it forms, and which general laws of nature it determines in the course of its inquiry. Still, this openness might seem to raise the question with added force: how can ideas prescribe an indeterminate and unattainable goal to all uses of the understanding?

4.2 Ideas As Rules for the Understanding

In many places, Kant explains this prescriptive force by claiming that ideas *serve as rules* for the understanding. So, I argue next that *a transcendental idea prescribes rules for the systematic extension of the use of the understanding in a specific domain of empirical reality*. In other words, ideas define meta-rules for how to apply the categories of the understanding in a certain domain. For example, Kant writes in his discussion of the Antinomies of Reason:

> Thus the principle of reason is *only a rule, prescribing a regress* in the series of conditions for given appearances. ... [I]t is *a principle of the greatest possible continuation and extension of experience* ... [A]n idea ... merely serves as a rule (A508/B536–A509/B537, emphasis added; see also A569/B597).

In the Appendix to the Dialectic, Kant specifies:

> an *idea* ... *serves as a rule for the way we ought to proceed in regard to them*: namely that in the explanation of given appearances (in a regress or ascent), we ought to proceed as if the series were in itself infinite, i.e., proceed *in indefinitum* (A685/B713, emphasis added; see also A663/B691).

---

[89] For example, ideas have 'objective but indeterminate validity' (A663/B691); the principle of systematic unity is 'objective but in an indeterminate way (*principium vagum*)'(A680/B708); 'The absolute totality of the series of these conditions in the derivation of their members is an idea which of course can never come about fully in the empirical use of reason' (A685/B713). Walden (2019: 582–588) helpfully stresses the indeterminacy of ideas – a point to which I return to in Subsections 4.3 and 5.3.

Kant's Ideas of Reason 45

Ideas thus give prescriptive rules for the understanding to proceed towards the 'greatest possible continuation and extension of experience' (A508/B536).[90] This greatest extension involves both the maximal extension of a system of empirical concepts and the maximal extension of a system of empirical cognitions (including laws of nature). Extending our cognition can include exploring further areas of space and time, finding more distant objects, or enlarging the scope of reality we can describe by laws. Extending our concepts can include – according to the three principles of concept-formation – homogeneity, specification, and continuity – defining a common genus-concept of a yet larger scope (e.g., organism), defining more fine-grained species-concepts (e.g., a subspecies of rose), or differentiating a concept from further neighbouring concepts (e.g., concepts of other flowers such as tulip and orchid).[91]

Kant frequently describes the extension of the understanding's use in terms of a 'continuous progression of the empirical synthesis' (A462/B490) by which the understanding combines sensible intuition according to its categories.[92] This extension can be 'a regress to the [higher, more general] conditions' of an appearance (A499/B527), the progression 'to a higher (more remote) member' (A518/B546) of the series, or the successive composition of spaces and times (see A500/B528). It can also be the 'decomposition [into] an unconditioned (indivisible) member of this series of conditions' such that 'the division goes to infinity' (A513/B541).[93]

The general account is, then, that the understanding must follow the guidance of reason, if it is to extend its use. Ideas provide rules for this systematic extension. The general rule is that ideas demand us to 'initiat[e] and continu[e] ... in the series of conditions for a given conditioned' (A508/B536).[94] The twist here is that the transcendental ideas supplement the three general formal principles of concept-formation: they specify how these formal principles are to be applied in a specific domain and thus how the empirical synthesis of the understanding is to be extended in that domain.

Let me explain with the example of the idea of the soul. The idea of a *simple substance* calls us to extend the empirical synthesis of our inner intuitions towards the sum total of inner appearances. We will never find this totality in experience, regardless of how far we extend the empirical synthesis. Nonetheless, this idea supplies a rule for how to make progress: we ought to

---

[90] Spagnesi (2023a) similarly emphasizes that reason provides 'meta-rules' to the understanding.
[91] See 2.3.   [92] See also A409/B436, A479/B507, A499/B527.
[93] For accounts of different kinds of series, see, e.g., Watkins (2019b), Falkenburg (2020), Rosefeldt (2021), Chaplin (2024).
[94] Spagnesi (2023a:680) discusses this principle as the 'Regulative Supreme Principle', i.e., a corrected version of the unqualified supreme principle of reason (see 2.2). On the demand for continued empirical synthesis, see also A515/B543, A520/B548.

cognize inner appearances *as if* they were mental states inhering in a mental substance, even though we cannot intuit such a substance. The idea of the soul gives rise to domain-specific rules for applying the categories of the understanding to the domain of psychological beings. In general, how a category of the understanding is applied in empirical cognition depends on the kind of whole that we aim to explore with it.[95]

Hence, there is a sense in which the *presupposition of the whole* precedes the prescription of the rules for the use of the understanding. The kind of whole presupposed specifies the kind of rules that can be derived. Ideas give rise to domain-specific rules by outlining the domain, or what I will call a *context of intelligibility*. This is the context in which a systematic use of the understanding is at all possible for us.

4.3 Ideas As Contexts of Intelligibility

Finally, I argue that ideas of reason provide a priori mental maps of the domains of reality in which the understanding can extend its use systematically. More specifically, *the regulative use of transcendental ideas outlines the context of intelligibility within which the understanding can make systematic progress by an indeterminately continued empirical synthesis.*

The following problem still lurks in the background: an idea prescribes a whole as the goal for the understanding's empirical syntheses – a goal, however, that must remain indeterminate from the standpoint of experience. There cannot be a determinate concept of this goal, nor can there be an actual 'empirical boundary' for the determining activities of the understanding that 'would hold as an absolute boundary' (A509/B537), as 'no experience is bounded absolutely' (A515/B543).[96] Rather, reason prescribes only 'a progress of indeterminate length (*progressus in indefinitum*)' (A511/B539) or 'a regress extending *indeterminately far (in indefinitum)*' (A512/B540).[97] But how can we derive rules for the determining activities of the understanding from an indeterminate goal?

The central point of the perspectivalist interpretation is this: ideas of reason provide the understanding with an a priori mapping or structuring of a domain

---

[95] For this example, see Kraus (2020, ch. 5), and Spagnesi (2023a:683). A crucial point of my interpretation in Kraus (2020) is that we cannot apply the category of substance to inner appearances as we do to outer appearances. The first analogy provides a principle for material substances in space. The idea of the soul supplies the corresponding principle for inner appearances (see the exchange between Frierson (2022) and Kraus (2022)).

[96] See also A326–327/B383.

[97] See also A518/B546, A520/B548, A685/B713. Note that Kant distinguishes the conceptual (philosophical) progress *in indefinitum* from the mathematical notion of continuing *in infinitum* (e.g., A510/B538); see Walden (2019).

of empirical reality, even though the boundary of this domain is indeterminate. Only by presupposing such an a priori mapping can the understanding 'locate' an object of a particular experience on the map and then determine it in relation to this mapping. For example, by presupposing the idea of absolute space, the understanding can place a material object on a spatial map and determine its motion in relation to this map. By presupposing the idea of the soul, the understanding can position a mental state within the temporal development of a psychological being and determine its causal effects within this development. This anchoring of an object within a map, spanned by an idea, must in a logical sense precede the determining activities of the understanding. Otherwise, no systematically coherent and inferentially connected cognition of the object can be achieved. The regulative use of an idea thus provides the understanding with what I call a *context of intelligibility*: an a priori map, outline, or sketch of a domain of empirical reality. An object can only become *intelligible* (or *comprehensible*) for us if an appropriate context of intelligibility is presupposed.[98] This requires that the experience of the object must be reflected under an appropriate idea. This idea generates a context within which the object can be cognized in relation to other objects within a systematic web of dependence relations. Without such a context, the cognition of the object would remain rhapsodic or fragmentary.

Let me provide textual and philosophical support for this reading. That reason provides something like a context of intelligibility is indicated in phrases such as that reason 'prepares the field for the understanding' (A657/B685), 'points the way toward systematic unity' (A668/B696), and 'open[s] up new paths into the infinite (the undetermined)' (A680/B708).

A key aspect of Kant's account, on my view, is that ideas specify an a priori structure of the field, even though they cannot determine its boundaries in an absolute or determinate way. The a priori structure concerns the kind of dependence relations in which the objects belonging to this context must stand (e.g., material causation vs. mental causation). That ideas give an a priori structure to a field of the understanding is, for example, indicated in the following passage:

> This unity of reason always presupposes an idea, namely that of *the form of a whole of cognition, which precedes the determinate cognition of the parts* and contains the conditions for determining a priori the place of each part and its relation to the others. (A645/B673, emphasis added)

---

[98] Kant frequently assigns the purpose of 'comprehension' to reason: 'Concepts of reason serve for *comprehension*, just as concepts of the understanding serve for *understanding* (of perceptions)' (A311/B367). Schafer (2023) develops a unified account of reason as the faculty of comprehension.

According to this passage, an idea provides the 'form of a whole of cognition' from which explanations for a given appearance can be derived. For example, the idea of absolute space gives the 'form of a whole' to the system of physics, so that an explanation of the trajectory of a material object can be obtained in terms of mechanical laws. An idea also defines the 'form of a whole' at the level of concepts: rather than being itself the 'concept of an object', it gives such concepts a 'thoroughgoing unity' by means of an a priori form (A645/B673).

Further evidence for the claim that ideas define an a priori structure comes from Kant's characterization of ideas as *schemata*, in analogy with the schemata of the understanding.[99] Without going into detail, I propose that this analogy can help us to understand how ideas – by defining a structured whole – provide rules for the understanding. As Kant writes:

> Thus the idea of reason is an *analogue of a schema of sensibility* [i.e., schema of the understanding], but with this difference, that the application of concepts of the understanding to the schema of reason is not likewise a cognition of the object itself (as in the application of the categories to their sensible schemata), but *only a rule or principle of the systematic unity of all use of the understanding.* (A665/B693, emphasis added)

In other places, Kant argues that the execution of any idea requires a schema that provides not only 'the outline (*monogramma*)' of the system the idea spans, but also 'the division of [its] members' and the 'order of [its] parts' (A833/B861, see also A682ff./B710ff.). This analogy between the schemata of the understanding and those of reason can be understood as follows: a schema of the understanding gives 'a rule for the determination of [the unity of] our intuition in accordance with a [category]' (A141/B180). Similarly, a 'schema of reason' gives 'a rule or principle of the systematic unity of all use of the understanding' in accordance with an idea (A665/B693). Both define procedural rules to attain some unity: in the former case, a rule to attain the unity of a manifold of intuition in accordance with a category; in the latter case, a rule to attain the systematic unity of manifold cognitions in accordance with an idea.

This analogy is difficult to work out, because it is controversial what exactly a schema is in the first instance.[100] In Kraus (2020:194–206), I offer a detailed discussion, highlighting the following point: the essential role of a schema is to make a concept sensible, that is, to provide an a priori *presentation* of a concept to the mind in a sensible form.[101] The schemata of the understanding are the

---

[99] On ideas as schemata, see A665/B693, A670/B698, A674/B702, A679/B707. Spagnesi's (2023a) 'rule-based account' is also based on this analogy.

[100] See, e.g., Allison (2004).

[101] In the *Critique of the Power of Judgment*, Kant defines a schema in terms of a 'presentation' (*Darstellung*), or as 'making something sensible' (CJ 5:351), as opposed to a *representation*

Kant's Ideas of Reason

sensible presentations of the conceptual unities defined by the categories and thus explicate the categories in sensible form (e.g., the category of substance is schematized as persistence in time). Likewise, the regulative use of an idea results in the *presentation* of the 'form of a whole' defined by the idea. Since, however, such a whole can never be fully sensibly instantiated, it can only be a *symbolic presentation*.[102] We can now understand the *presupposition of a whole* involved in the regulative use of ideas in terms of an a priori act of *presentation* to the mind.

This presentation of a whole is what I mean by generating a context of intelligibility. The mind produces an internal map, as it were, of empirical reality for the guidance and orientation of the understanding. The context of intelligibility is thus a *mental presentation of empirical reality* as a structured whole, or simply of *nature* as the 'sum total of appearances' (e.g., B163, A257/B312, A418–419/B446n, A674/B702). This mental presentation outlines the maximal domain in which the understanding can systematically operate to determine given appearances. In presenting this domain to the mind a priori, reason produces procedural rules for how to approach systematic unity within this domain.

So, we can now understand the rules defined by an idea as rules for the *relational determination* of objects of cognition against the a priori mapping that the idea provides. Several passages indicate this relational significance of ideas:[103]

> Reason . . . only *orders* [concepts (of objects)] and gives them that unity . . . *in relation to the totality of series*; the understanding does not look to this totality at all, but only to *the connection through which series* of conditions always *come about* according to concepts. (A643/B671, emphasis added)

> we think *a relation to the sum total of appearances*, which is *analogous to the relation that appearances have to one another*. (A674/B702, emphasis added)

An idea defines the relational structure between a whole and its parts: primarily between a system of concepts and individual concepts, but also between a system of cognitions and the individual cognitions contained in it. If our cognitive activities are successful, then this relational structure should also be reflected in the domain of reality captured by a system of cognitions and give

---

(*Vorstellung*) (see Kraus 2020:197–198). Kant also uses the notions *exhibitionis* and *hypotyposis*, indicating the meaning of a 'model', 'sketch', or 'outline'.

[102] On the need for symbolization in the use of ideas, see also Maly (2011), Breitenbach (2014), and Nassar (2016).

[103] See also A670/B698, A677/B705, A700/B728. This might be what Adickes (1924:82–83) means by the 'relative significance' of things-in-themselves, which is productive for the cognition of objects, in contrast to their 'absolute significance', which leads to transcendental fallacies.

order to the appearances that belong to this domain. The significance of ideas is thus only relational and concerns the ordering of empirical concepts and cognitions (and their corresponding appearances) according to dependence relations within a whole. With this relational significance ideas contribute to determining conceptual content: the relational structures they define 'make it possible for us to be able to have a determinate concept of any thing' in the first place (A674/B702).

This can perhaps be made plausible by comparing the context of intelligibility with the linguistic conception of a *context of use*, which inspired my terminology. A context of use, in which a certain linguistic expression is used, has a content-determining function. For example, the indexicals 'I', 'here', or 'now' have a definite content only in a context of use (i.e., the relevant set of states of affairs) in which these indexicals refer to something particular, namely the speaker, place, or time of the context, respectively.[104] Similarly, I suggest, the context of intelligibility has a content-enabling function: the empirical content of a concept is only sufficiently defined against the background of a whole system of concepts, which can be mapped onto a domain of reality. To have a sufficient grasp of what a concept means (i.e., sufficient for a particular purpose) requires a sufficient insight into the conceptual entailment relations it has to other concepts within a system.[105] Similarly, the content of a cognition is understood in terms of inferential relations it has to other cognitions within a system. These relations are supposed to capture the real conditioning relations in nature, or the sum total of appearances.

Let me illustrate this with an example. The idea of natural purposiveness can now be understood to outline the context of intelligibility for the study of living nature. It defines the form of the system of biological concepts with the highest genus-concept <organism>, as schematically shown in Figure 4. This system is supposed to map onto the domain of reality in which we can at all hope to identify organic beings, that is, the 'living world'.[106] The idea moreover supplies the rules for identifying the parts of an organism (e.g., its organs) in relation to the whole.[107] Without presupposing this idea, I would not be able to interpret the rose I intuit as an organic whole and identify its parts as contributing to its organic life (e.g., its stem, petals, thorns, etc.).

---

[104] There are various accounts of a context of use; a plausible one is offered by Kaplan (1989).
[105] In the *Jäsche-Logic*, Kant emphasizes that the insight of human reason is only ever 'sufficient for our purpose' (JL 9:65).
[106] See Breitenbach (2014:133).
[107] A growing number of publications argue that for Kant the very conception of an organism presupposes the idea of purposiveness, which then enables the mechanical explanations of organic parts, e.g., Breitenbach (2014), Nassar (2016), Geiger (2022). At the same time, reason instructs us to seek further conditions: in modern biology, the mechanisms of genetics and natural selection.

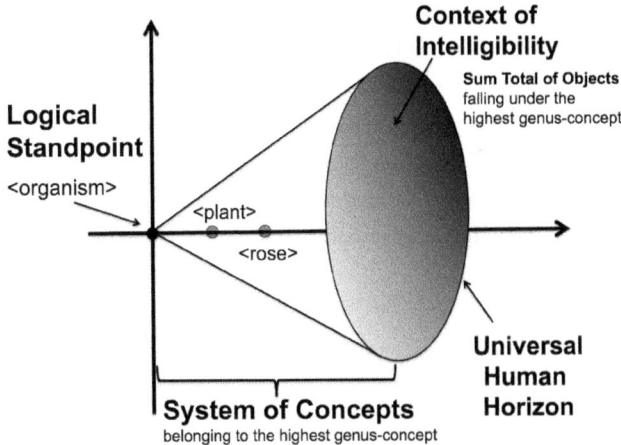

Figure 4 Schematic account of the conceptual system of biological terms, spanned by the genus-concept <organism>.

To sum up, I have argued that the regulative use of ideas can be understood as outlining or sketching the contexts of intelligibility within which the understanding can be extended in a systematic way, in the hope of finding a systematic conceptualization of the empirical world and a system of inferential cognitions. A context of intelligibility is the mental presentation of empirical reality as a structured whole, which is assumed to correspond to the sum total of appearances, or simply to nature. This presentation must be presupposed a priori in any specific determination of an empirical object. It is a mental map for the understanding to advance to the greatest extension and the greatest specification of its concepts and thus approach the most detailed description of nature according to general laws. Ideas do not outline the domain of the understanding by determining its boundaries in an absolute or even only hypothetical way. Rather, ideas give an a priori inner structure to a domain, from which domain-specific rules for the continued empirical synthesis of the understanding follow. Without presupposing this a priori structured whole, objects would remain unintelligible for us. The perspectivalist view thus accounts for the fact that ideas set a priori limits to what is empirically cognizable in certain domains.[108] But the view also allows for an infinite process of revision and expansion of empirical concepts and cognitions.[109]

---

[108] In the *Prolegomena*, ideas are considered not only to 'set limits (*Schranken*)' to reason's pretensions, but also to 'determine' these limits as 'boundaries (*Grenzen*)' of reason's empirical use (see P 4:350–354). Callanan (2021, esp. 148) concludes from this that ideas serve to represent the boundaries of a domain of possible experience.

[109] For an opposite view, see Walden's (2019) diagnosis that from the indeterminacy of the boundaries it follows that reason itself is unbound.

Since the transcendental ideas of reason are due to the nature of human reason, they are shared among all humans and open up common contexts of intelligibility. These ideas delineate the empirical reality to be cognized from the *human perspective*. The perspectivalist interpretation thus offers a natural reading of the visual metaphors discussed in Subsection 3.1: an idea, as the highest standpoint of the human perspective, opens up the universal human horizon (see A659/B687). This universal horizon encompasses all commonly shared contexts of intelligibility.

4.4 Ideas Set Topics for the Understanding: Natural Kinds

In many places, reason is described as *setting a task* or *problem* for the understanding to be completed.[110] The perspectivalist interpretation gives this description a further twist by suggesting that reason *sets topics* for the understanding to explore. Ideas not only outline the a priori structures of domains of reality, but also define the *kinds of objects* that the understanding can hope to find in these domains. These are the *natural kinds* that can at all be intelligible for us. In particular, I argue that the transcendental ideas of the soul and the world-whole define the most general *natural kinds* that the understanding is demanded to explore in nature. I focus on the idea of the soul and the idea of absolute space.

Consider Kant's specification of the idea of the *soul*: it contains the predicates (or sub-ideas) of 'a simple substance, unchangeable in itself (identical in personality), standing in community with other real things outside it' (A682/B710). I must presuppose this idea to derive 'principles of the systematic unity in explaining the appearances of the soul' (A682/B710) (or what Kant also calls *inner appearances*). The predicates of the soul give rise to such principles by

> considering all determinations as in one subject, all powers, as far as possible, as derived from one unique fundamental power, all change as belonging to the states of one and the same persisting being, and by representing all *appearances* in space as entirely distinct from the actions of *thinking*. (A682/B710–A683/B711)

On the perspectivalist view, the idea of the soul generates a context of intelligibility for a particular kind of experience (i.e., inner experience) and defines the object that can be determined within this context (i.e., inner appearances). For various reasons, we cannot cognize ourselves as mental substances, since the principle of substantiality applies primarily to material objects.[111] The idea of the soul nonetheless provides the appropriate context for explaining inner

---

[110] See A287/B344, A323/B380, A327/B384, A335/B392, A498/B526, A508/B536, A647/B675, A657/B685, A669/B697.

[111] See Kraus (2020) and (2022), and Frierson (2022), and fn. 95.

appearances in a systematic way and gives regulative rules for applying the principles of the understanding specifically to inner appearances. The principles require us to determine inner appearances as the mental states of a substance that persists through time, as states caused by mental faculties that are all grounded in a single fundamental power, and as states that are correlated with a body (without, however, determining a mental substance as a whole). These principles define the a priori structure of the context in which inner appearances can be explained: they can be explained only in relation to the sum total that makes up a person's mental life. The idea of the soul thus sets a topic for us: we ought to explore psychological beings through the inner relation of their inner appearances to an assumed substantial whole.[112]

Another example is the idea of the *world in space*, which is a sub-idea of the world-whole. It plays a central role in Kant's account of mechanics: only if we presuppose an idea of absolute space can we define a frame of reference in relation to which mechanical motion can be cognized in accordance with Newton's laws of motion.[113] Following the perspectivalist interpretation, the regulative function of this idea is then to define the domain of physics within which Newton's laws are valid for material objects. But the Dialectic has taught us that the idea of the world in space involves an antinomy: we must think of the spatial world as both an infinite whole without boundaries and a finite whole with boundaries.[114] So if we try to determine the spatial world as an unconditioned object, we cannot avoid this contradiction. We cannot even think of space as an *object in the idea*, that is, as a substance that logically precedes its accidents (see A673/B702). Rather, the context opened by the idea of absolute space is structured as a *composition* of subspaces, whereby the subspaces logically precede the whole they compose.[115] The idea of absolute space thus sets a different topic for us: we ought to explore material beings through their external relations to one another in an assumed compositional whole.

From these two examples, I draw broader conclusions: the two classes of ideas – the ideas of the soul and of the world-whole – define the two fundamental kinds of context-structures (substantial vs. compositional whole) and the two

---

[112] For details, see Kraus (2020, ch. 5) and Kraus (2018). Grier (2001) and Dyck (2014) recognize the importance of the idea for defining the domain of psychology.

[113] I take it that the idea of absolute space in the *Metaphysical Foundations of Natural Science* (MFNS 4:559) corresponds to the idea of the world in space in the first *Critique*. For discussion, see Friedman (2013:437ff.).

[114] See First Antinomy (A426/B454–A433/B461). Unlike the soul and God, the world cannot be represented as a totality without contradiction (see A677/B705). Antinomies arise from the cosmological ideas, e.g., the third antinomy regarding causality, which oscillates between the idea of causal necessity and that of spontaneous freedom (see A444ff./B472ff.). See Posy (1983), Falkenburg (2020), Hogan (2021), Howard (2022a, 2022b, 2024).

[115] See A161/B203, A415/B443.

corresponding most general *natural kinds* that we can hope to find in nature at all.[116] Any object we seek to cognize falls under one of the two kinds. From the two kinds of systematic unities (soul-like substantial wholes or world-like compositional wholes), we can derive two natural kinds: soul-like (or animate) objects and material objects. Soul-like objects are defined by their inner unity, which precedes their parts, and by the internal relations that their parts have to the whole.[117] For example, a mental state is determined in relation to the whole person, and mental causation is understood to be exercised by the person as a whole. Material objects, by contrast, are defined by their external relations to other objects, which together form a compositional spatial whole. A material part is primarily defined by its relation to other material parts. Mechanical forces are exerted by mass particles on each other, not by space as a whole. Biological organisms are a hybrid case because they fall under both types: organic parts are understood as functions of the whole organism, and yet we seek mechanical explanations for them in terms of their parts.[118]

The perspectivalist interpretation suggests that reason sets topics for the understanding to explore in nature. An idea of reason defines a 'sketch of a science', which is given as a 'problem' (A335/B392). The ideas of the soul and the world-whole, in particular, are indispensable for exploring the domains of animate and of inanimate nature.[119]

5 The Perspectivalist Interpretation: Ultimate Reality As *Focus Imaginarius*

Finally, the question remains as to why it is legitimate at all to use ideas of reason to systematically extend the grasp of the understanding. How can we make sure that they do not lead us astray but instead enable real progress in the cognition of nature? The normative bindingness of ideas may only be justified if

---

[116] This proposal is similar to the views offered by Spagnesi (2023a, 2023b), in terms of phenomenal essences, Hoffer (2019, 2023), in terms of regulative essences, and Massimi (2021), in terms of natural kinds. Ideas such as 'pure earth, pure water, pure air, etc.' (A646/B674) may also define natural kinds. Since they are not *transcendental* ideas, they do not define the limits of experience, nor do they outline nature as the sum total of appearances. For example, the 'idea of a mechanism' applied to the 'chemical effects of materials' (A646/B674) defines the domain of chemical matter; see McNulty (2015).

[117] In the first *Critique*, Kant reserves 'soul' specifically for thinking beings. In the *Critique of the Power of Judgment*, Kant develops a broader notion of 'soul' in terms of 'the idea of natural purposiveness', which refers more broadly to living beings and accords with the Aristotelian tradition of 'psyche' (ψυχή), often translated as 'anima' in Kant's Latin terminology.

[118] See Geiger (2022).

[119] On the distinction between the outer, extended, or bodily nature and inner, or thinking, nature, see A846/B874, MFNS 4:469. On ideas of sciences, see Sturm (2009) and Kraus (2018, 2023). In the Appendix, by contrast, the idea of the world-whole concerns both 'the inner as well as the outer appearances of nature' (A672/B700, also A684f./B712f.).

it can be assumed that they are grounded in an 'ultimate reality' that guarantees such real progress.[120] Recall that this was the major advantage of noumenalism over fictionalism (see 1.5). The perspectivalist view, as it has been presented so far, could still be considered a fictionalist view, denying that ideas refer to anything real *beyond* the human horizon (see 1.6). In what follows, I argue that the perspectivalist view needs to be completed by an argument for the ideas' legitimacy (and objective validity). Kant aims to provide such an argument with the transcendental deduction of ideas in the Appendix. This argument sheds light on the second role of ideas for the normative assessment of truth.

Subsection 5.1 raises a worry about the possibility of assessing the success of empirical cognition of nature. Subsection 5.2 shows that this worry can be dispelled by Kant's conception of God: the regulative use of the idea of God grounds the principle that all things in nature are completely determined (as argued in the Transcendental Ideal (TI) chapter of the Dialectic). This *principle of thoroughgoing determination* (PTD) is a necessary condition for the possibility of evaluating the truth of cognition. Subsection 5.3 proposes that ideas of reason provide normative ideals for truth-evaluation by projecting an ultimate reality (as is shown in their transcendental deductions). These projections serve as what I call ultimate circumstances of evaluation, that is, broadly speaking, the states of the world that make a cognition true or in virtue of which a cognition is true.[121] This ultimate reality can be considered as the world as it is in itself or simply without being viewed from a perspective. For finite beings like us, however, this world must remain a *focus imaginarius*.

5.1 Assessing the Empirical Use of the Understanding

How can we make sure that our efforts for a systematic conceptualization and cognition of appearances are really successful?[122] How can we assess whether we make progress towards systematic, complete, and indeed true descriptions and explanations of objects in nature? We must grant that empirical concepts and empirical laws are ever revisable and extendable. But how then can we judge whether an empirical law of nature that we have discovered is actually true, or at least approximates universal validity? How can we judge whether a cognition in fact tracks real dependence relations between (or within) the object(s) it describes?[123]

---

[120] See van Inwagen (2008:1). For discussion in relation to Kant, see Stang (forthcoming).
[121] Following Kaplan (1989), I distinguish the circumstances of evaluation from the context of use (i.e., in my view, the context of intelligibility). See also Spohn (2016) and Lewis (1980).
[122] Kant attests that ideas facilitate such success, as they 'can even be used with good success, as heuristic principles' (A663/B691). On the incompleteness of the understanding, see 2.1.
[123] Kreines (2017) argues that, for Kant, we can never know laws of nature from an empirical standpoint. For opposite views, see Geiger (2022) and Spagnesi (2023b). Each view seems compatible with the quest for evaluation criteria for empirical laws of nature.

In Subsection 2.2, we saw that reason's demand for systematic unity provides a 'touchstone' (A647/B675) or 'mark of empirical truth' (A651/B679). Since we cannot judge independently of our representations whether a cognition really corresponds to an object of experience, as Kant's correspondence theory of truth requires, we have to use criteria of systematicity to evaluate the truth of empirical cognitions. So, I argued that Kant advocates a *systematicity theory of truth-criteria*:[124] The truth of a cognition is judged in terms of its systematic relations to other cognitions already accepted as true.[125] The fit of a cognition within a system of cognitions entails that it does not contradict any cognitions already accepted as true; it arguably also entails its derivability from higher-order principles. Does this systematic fit provide objectively sufficient grounds for assenting the cognition, that is, grounds that are valid in light of the object?[126]

This raises a fundamental worry: if the demands of reason for systematicity guide the way we form empirical concepts and gain systematically connected cognition, then nature will simply present itself to us according to the systematic conceptualization we have put into the cognition of nature. But if we in turn use systematicity as a measure of the progress we have made in approaching a complete and true description of nature, we might only ever measure the subjective systematizing efforts we have put into that description, following our formal principles of reason, rather than the objective progress we have really made in light of nature itself. So, we lack an objective standard for judging progress that is independent of our own subjective demands for systematization. Put differently, there may be a problem of circularity if we use reason's own principles of systematicity both to extend the use of the understanding and to assess the *correctness* of that use. Let me explore this worry further before turning to Kant's solution based on the idea of God.

Consider the formal and the material definition of nature in the Antinomies chapter:

> "Nature" taken adjectivally (*formaliter*) signifies the connection of determinations of a thing in accordance with an inner principle of causality. Conversely, by "nature" taken substantively (*materialiter*) is understood the

---

[124] This may be considered as a version of a coherence theory of justification. Coherence, however, may have lower requirements than systematicity. On coherence as a condition of knowledge for Kant, see Chignell (2014).

[125] Empirical truth, for Kant, can be 'secured' if appearances can be shown to be 'correctly and thoroughly connected up according to empirical laws in one experience' (A492/B520–521). This may require that some empirical laws are evident simply through perception. For an evidentialist reading, see Posy (1981).

[126] Objectively sufficient assent is a condition of knowledge, see Chignell (2007b) and Watkins and Willaschek (2020). But I set aside more specific questions about knowledge.

sum total of appearances insofar as these are in *thoroughgoing connection* through an inner principle of causality. (A418–419n/B446n, emphasis added)[127]

According to its formal definition, nature is necessarily structured according to an 'inner principle of causality'. The Transcendental Analytic has shown that the principle of causality is applicable to all appearances. As a transcendental principle, it gives rise to a formal order in which appearances must be formally related to each other to be cognizable at all. Yet if we consider nature in terms of its matter according to its material definition, it could still turn out to be 'a raw chaotic aggregate' of appearances without showing 'the least trace of a system' (FI 20:209). We have no guarantee a priori that, if we apply the formal principle of causality to all appearances, they will constitute a systematic whole in which all appearances are really in a 'thoroughgoing [causal] connection' with each other. That is, the real thoroughgoing determination of appearances is not guaranteed, as we will see in 5.2.

Kant considers the extreme case that nature simply does not display systematic connections and therefore does not lend itself to the kind of systematic description that reason demands. Kant entertains the possibility that there could be 'such a great variety ... of content, i.e., regarding the manifoldness of existing beings ... that even the most acute human understanding ... could not detect the least similarity' (A653/B681). However, if this were the case, then not only could there be 'no concept of a genus, nor any other universal concept', but also 'indeed no understanding at all'; that is, 'no empirical concepts and hence no experience would be possible' for us (A654/B682). This argument from the possibility of infinite variety leads Kant to conclude that the principle of homogeneity must have a transcendental status and is thus objectively valid with regard to nature itself.[128]

If we are guided by the transcendental, albeit regulative principles of systematicity, they guarantee a priori that we form empirical concepts to reflect systematic conditioning relations of genus and species, at least to some degree. On this basis we then acquire empirical cognitions that stand in systematic conditioning relations to one another so that we can draw further inferences from them. Hence, nature – if viewed only regarding its *form* – presents itself to us in such a way that it satisfies reason's demand for systematicity. But since

---

[127] See also B161–163, MFNS 4:467.
[128] For discussion, see Spagnesi (2023a) and 2.3. Kant offers analogous arguments for the transcendental status of the principles of specification and continuity. In the *Critique of the Power of Judgment*, Kant concedes that principles of systematicity are only 'subjectively necessary' (FI 20:209) and seems to give up on their objective validity. On the relation between the first *Critique* and the third *Critique*, see, e.g., Guyer (1990), Zuckert (2007) and Geiger (2022).

these transcendental principles are not constitutive of nature as a whole, we do *not* have an a priori guarantee that we *empirically* succeed in finding highest genus-concepts or lower, more specific species-concepts, or that there is always another concept between two neighbouring concepts. For example, we might see more hues of a colour than we can distinguish conceptually.

The same applies with regard to completeness. Formally speaking, the transcendental deduction shows that *all* appearances necessarily stand under the categories of the understanding. It follows that all appearances that make up nature as their sum total are objects of possible experience and thus cognizable. If we systematically extend the empirical use of the understanding, it is a priori guaranteed that no appearance in principle eludes our capacity for cognition, even if we fail to access many appearances, lack actual intuitions, or fail to grasp certain aspects of nature under systematic laws. However, nature taken in its material completeness might not be an actually infinite totality or representable as a systematic whole.[129]

Back to the problem of truth-evaluation. Again, if we follow reason's principles of concept-formation, we are guaranteed a priori that the empirical concepts we use in cognition stand in logical conditioning relations. But it can only be assessed a posteriori in light of actual experience whether these conceptual relations correspond to real dependence relations in the objects of experience to be described.[130] For example, we can only examine empirically whether objects that fall under the concept <rose> also instantiate predicates such as <have five petals> or <have a stem with thorns>, which are not analytically contained in <rose>. But how do we decide whether an exception we find, for example a rose that has no thorns or only three petals, is in fact a misapplication of <rose> or a counterexample to the systematic connection we established between <rose> and <have a stem with thorns>, or between <rose> and <have five petals>?

Now, how can systematicity be an indicator of empirical truth at all, as Kant claims? Can we measure the degree of systematicity that a newly acquired concept (or cognition) adds to the system of concepts (or cognitions)?

Taking a cue from the convergence of infinite series in mathematics, we can distinguish between an internal and an external measure for systematicity.[131] An

---

[129] Chaplin (2024) presents a strong argument that only unconditioned wholes can be actual infinities, but that nature as the sum total of conditioned appearances might not be.

[130] Similar to the argument for the transcendental principle of homogeneity, Kant argues that empirical truth presupposes 'the systematic unity of nature as objectively valid and necessary' (A651/B679). That nature is systematic is an a priori necessary but not sufficient condition of truth (see 2.2).

[131] The terms 'internal' and 'external' here mean *internal* and *external* to the relevant system or to the human mind.

external measure would measure the degree of systematicity in a system by its convergence to its limit, which is an external value, similar to a mathematical series that converges to a certain number, such as $\sum_{n=0}^{\infty} \frac{1}{2^n} = 2$. An internal measure, by contrast, would measure systematicity not against its limit, but by comparing the elements of the system to one another. In our case, this could be in terms of an increase in the density between concepts or in the scope of a conceptual system, regardless of whether the system as a whole approaches an external limit, that is, a mind-independent reality.[132]

Now, if we judge the degree of systematicity internally, we run the risk of measuring only the systematization efforts we have put into the system. We might measure the systematicity among cognitions only in terms of the logical conditioning relations between concepts we stipulated but miss out on the dependence relations that really exist in nature. In other words, we might be in a *frictionless spinning in the void* without testing our cognitions against the resistance of reality.[133] If, however, we use an external standard, we would require something like a given external value against which we can measure the convergence of the whole system. But we have no access to an external reality that is independent of the system of cognitions in the relevant sense.[134]

In what follows, I suggest that Kant offers a solution to the problem of truth-evaluation based on the idea of God. This idea must be presupposed in the empirical study of nature, since it enables the ideal of an external measure of truth.

5.2 The Idea of God As a Normative Standard

More than any other idea, Kant associates the idea of God with the notion of perfection. The idea is, for example, associated with the notion of 'complete purposive unity', which is identified with 'perfection' (A694/B722). The purpose of this idea 'is to serve us as the standard [*Richtschnur*] for the empirical use of reason' (A674–675/B702–703), and it is therefore 'legislative for us' (A695/B723). Early in his discussion of ideas of reason, Kant introduces a comparison with Plato: a Platonic idea defines 'what is most perfect of its species'; for example, 'the idea of humanity' defines what is most perfect for human beings (A318/B374). So far, the ideas of the soul and the world-whole have been understood as ideas of *human* reason, which outline the human

---

[132] In mathematics, for example, Cauchy's convergence test measures convergence internally. I thank Nick Stang for drawing my attention to this mathematical comparison.
[133] See McDowell (1994:11).
[134] Truth-bearers, for Kant, are primarily cognitions and judgements. Truth is not defined for an entire system of cognitions, which may not even have a corresponding object or referent. See Melamedoff-Vosters (2022:43–46).

horizon. But following Plato, Kant now considers the ideas that a *divine* intellect might have, which he calls *ideals*. An ideal is, like the Platonic '*idea in the divine understanding*', understood as 'the most perfect thing of each species of possible beings' (A568/B596). Importantly, with this shift towards the divine intellect, ideas of reason are assigned a new function: they do not only provide rules for extending and refining the understanding's systematic use within the human horizon, but, as ideals, they also serve as an 'indispensable standard [*Richtmaß*] for reason' (A569/B597):

> the ideal ... serves as the original image for the thoroughgoing determination of the copy; and we have in us no other *standard [Richtmaß] for our actions* than the conduct of this divine human being, with which we can compare ourselves, judging ourselves and thereby improving ourselves, even though we can never reach the standard. (A569/B597, emphasis added)

> [ideals] provide an *indispensable standard for reason*, which needs the concept of that which is entirely complete in its kind, in order to *assess and measure the degree and the defects of what is incomplete*. (A569/B597–A570/B598, emphasis added)

Hence, specifically the idea of God fulfils the function of cultivating our cognitive activities and assessing their 'correctness [*Richtigkeit*]' (A680/B708, see also A671/B699). It enables us to at least think of a normative standard that is not derived from human reason, but from the regulative idea of a divine intellect, an '*intellectus archetypus*' (A695/B723). What a divine intellect gives, *if* it exists, is an archetype, that is, an '*original image*' or 'original ground of all its copies in appearance' (A569/B597). It is a kind of storehouse for perfect things against which we can measure the faint empirical copies that appear to us.

While I cannot do justice to the large body of literature on this topic, I offer an interpretation of the idea of God in line with the perspectivalist interpretation. In the Appendix, Kant claims to provide a transcendental deduction for its objective validity: this deduction is supposed to show that the idea of God is a 'regulative principle of [the] investigation of nature' (A697/B725). Before I discuss the transcendental deduction in Subsection 5.3, I turn to the Transcendental Ideal (TI) in the Dialectic and highlight its relevance for the problem of truth-evaluation.[135]

The argument for the TI (A571/B599–A591/B619) appeals to the principle of thoroughgoing determination (PTD). This principle is crucial for the possibility of truth and definite reference of empirical cognition: it defines the state of the

---

[135] Important recent studies of the TI include Grier (2001), Allison (2004), Longuenesse (2005), and Willaschek (2018). Ypi (2021) offers a reading of the idea of God in the Appendix. Hoffer (2019) and Spagnesi (2022) offer compelling accounts of the role of this idea for the study of nature.

world in which a thing is fully determined with regard to all its possible properties. I contend that this state is what makes a cognition true and gives it a definite reference to a completely determined individual. Without reconstructing the argument in detail, I show how the TI can offer us further insight into Kant's solution to the problem highlighted in 5.1.[136] Recall that the problem is to explain how systematicity, although a regulative principle of reason, can provide an objective standard for evaluating truth and assessing the real progress made in the cognition of nature.

Even though truth is not explicitly discussed in the argument, the passage defines a logical and a material condition for truth.[137] First, a cognition has a definite truth-value only if the concepts used in it satisfy the *logical principle of determinability* (PD): 'that of every two contradictorily opposed predicates only one can apply to [the concept]' (A571/B599). For this logical principle to be applicable to empirical cognition, it requires the *transcendental principle of thoroughgoing determination* (PTD), 'according to which, among all possible predicates of things, insofar as they are compared with their opposites, one must apply to it' (A571–572/B599–600). Put in a more formal way:

(PTD) For every object x and for every possible predicate F_i: (either $F_i(x)$ or non-$F_i(x)$)

In further steps, the argument shows that PTD requires that there is 'the sum total of all [positive] predicates' (A573/B601), which is thought through 'the idea of an All of reality (*omnitudo realitatis*)' (A575/B603). This idea, then, leads Kant in a last step to the concept of the '*ens realissimum*', which is the concept of the 'individual being' that is 'the ground of the thoroughgoing determination' of all reality (A576/B604). This is simply the idea of God.[138] As several commentators convincingly show, the ideas of the *All of reality* and of the *ens realissimum* must be restricted to a regulative use.[139] A constitutive use would lead to transcendental illusions, in particular the 'hypostatization' of the ideas into really existing things (see A583/B611).

In consequence, PTD must be restricted to appearances and empirical predicates:

(PTD*) Now an *object of sense* can be thoroughly determined only if it is compared with all the *predicates of appearance* and is represented through them either affirmatively or negatively (A581/B609, emphasis added).

---

[136] Helpful reconstructions can be found in Willaschek (2018:218–231) and Spagnesi (2022).
[137] Truth is occasionally mentioned in the discussion, e.g., A492/B520-1 (see fn. 125).
[138] See Willaschek (2018:225–226).
[139] See esp. Longuenesse (2005), Willaschek (2018), and Spagnesi (2022). I follow Spagnesi's (2022) regulative qualifications regarding the idea of the *All of reality* and the idea of the *ens realissimum*.

PTD* presupposes that there is the 'sum total of empirical reality' (A582/B610), that is, *nature* as the sum total of appearances. The existence of nature as a systematic unity can only be guaranteed if we are justified in presupposing 'an individual thing' that is (or contains) the *determining real ground* of nature (A582/B610).[140] This leads Kant to define the TI as

> (TI) the ground of the thoroughgoing determination that is necessarily encountered in everything existing (A576/B604).

As such ground, TI is 'the supreme and complete *material* condition of [nature's] possibility' as a systematic whole (A576/B604, emphasis added). If it were to exist, TI would guarantee that nature – viewed materially – would be a systematic whole.[141] However, the argument for TI is not meant to show the 'existence of a being conforming to the ideal' (A577–578/B605–606). Rather, we can only assume TI and hence the idea of such a being, viz. God, *regulatively* (see A578/B606).

What does this imply for our problem of truth-evaluation? The idea of God must be assumed regulatively as the *sufficient material* condition for all objects in nature to be completely determinable. The assumption of a complete determination is a necessary condition for the cognition of an object to have a definite truth-value. The idea of God thus legitimizes our assumption that every cognition can be assessed against an objective standard of truth. What its regulative qualification amounts to becomes clear only in the Appendix, to which I now turn.

5.3 Ideas As Projections of a World without Perspective

Based on these considerations regarding the idea of God, I now argue that ideas of reason have their legitimacy with regard to the cognition of nature only as *normative ideals*. These ideals are projections of an ultimate reality beyond the human horizon. This is the reality against which we *should* measure the success of our cognition, *if* there were such a reality. But such a projection cannot itself amount to a truth-assessable assertion about such a reality. It can only ever be a *focus imaginarius* for us. The normative function of ideas is thus captured by this third visual metaphor (see 3.2).

Support for my argument is provided in Kant's transcendental deduction of the three ideas – the soul, the world-whole, and God – in the Appendix.

---

[140] On God as the determining real ground of reality, see Stang (2016:36–42, 307–313).
[141] The problem of whether nature, as the sum total of appearances, is an actual infinite totality, which I flagged in 5.1, is echoed in Kant's worry that we may 'hypostatize' the transcendental ideal into a being if we transform nature, as 'the *distributive* unity of the use of the understanding in experience', into the '*collective* unity of a whole' (A582/B610). See fn.129, Longuenesse (2005:222) and Spagnesi (2022:285–286).

Kant's Ideas of Reason 63

Kant concedes that ideas cannot be shown to have the same kind of objective validity as the categories, since no corresponding intuition can be given.[142] However, ideas are said to have 'objective but indeterminate validity' (A663/B691), or to be 'valid, albeit only indirectly, for the object of experience' (A665/B693). One way to understand this indirect (or indeterminate) objective validity is to accept that ideas do not establish positive claims about nature, as the categories do about objects of experience. Rather, in a negative sense, they define restrictions on nature: they project ideals without which nature could not be intelligible to us at all. If cognition were not 'cultivated and corrected' against these ideals, it could not be asserted as true (A671/B699; see 2.2).

In the transcendental deduction, Kant specifies that an idea has objective validity in terms of an 'object in the idea', rather than by being instantiated by a real thing (A670/B698, A671/B699, A697/B725). Positing an object in the idea, I argue, generates a normative ideal or standard for judging the correctness of cognition. Regarding the idea of God, Kant explicitly writes:

> For that we posit a thing corresponding to the idea [of God] ... only in the idea ... to express the systematic unity which is to serve us as the standard [*Richtschnur*] for the empirical use of reason (A674/B702-A675/B703).

Together with my argument about the TI in 5.2, we can now understand the regulative use of the idea of God as the positing of an object in the idea: we posit in the idea 'a substratum, unknown to us, of the systematic unity, order, and purposiveness of the world's arrangement' (A696/B724). This positing is not a conceptual determination, or an assertion, of such a substratum as an existing thing, as assumed by some noumenalists. Rather, it is the projection of an ultimate goal of our cognitive efforts.[143] The regulative use of the idea of God enables the projection of an ultimate reality that would ground the world of appearances. An ultimate reality is what would make the cognition of appearances true, independently of the way we carve up nature by our a priori forms and our empirical concepts.

The projection must remain an 'imagined object' (A670/B698) and as such a *focus imaginarius*. Recall that ideas of reason

---

[142] Kant first denies the possibility of a transcendental deduction (at A663/B691). It is controversial whether such a deduction can be successful (e.g., Ciami 1995) or not (e.g., McLaughlin 2014).

[143] Kant uses the terms 'postulating' (e.g., A645/B673, A650/B678) and 'positing' (e.g., A644/B672, A674/B702), which are opposed to 'hypostatizing' objects, i.e., 'making thoughts into things' (A395; also A582/B610, A619/B647). The transcendental deduction is meant to show that from positing an object in the idea, we can derive regulative principles that then serve as schemata, as explained in 4.3. If successful, the transcendental deduction would prove these schemata to be objectively valid.

> direct[] the understanding to a certain goal respecting which the lines of direction of all its rules converge at one point ... [This point] is only an idea (*focus imaginarius*) – i.e., a point from which the concepts of the understanding do not really proceed, since it lies entirely outside the bounds of possible experience (A644/B672).

A visual *focus imaginarius* is an illusory point 'behind the surface of a mirror' (A644/B672) from which an object seems to emerge. Similarly, an idea is a *focus imaginarius* from which 'an object lying outside the field of possible empirical cognition' (A644/B672) seems to appear. This focal point thus stands in for a reality that lies outside the world of appearances but that is assumed to ground appearances. To project this focal point imaginatively is indispensably necessary 'to take the measure of [the understanding's] greatest possible and uttermost extension' (A645/B673). That is, the focal point is required as an ideal standard for measuring our progress in finding systematic connections among appearances.

In the mirror case, we take an object behind the mirror to be the source of the image in the mirror. Similarly, we take an ultimate reality 'behind' the world of appearances to contain its ground. Even if we cannot prove that this ultimate reality exists 'absolutely and in itself as something actual' (A681/B709), we must project it. These projections are such that we can '*consider* all experiential cognition *as determined* through an absolute totality of conditions' (A327/B384, emphasis added), that is, through an ultimate reality. In contrast to strong fictionalism, however, these projections are not arbitrary fictions or 'mere figments of the brain' (A569/B597), but placeholders for an ultimate reality.

This ultimate reality, which must be assumed not to be conditioned by the human mind, might be identified with what Kant calls *things-in-themselves*.[144] Without taking a stance on the many thorny questions about things-in-themselves and their relation to appearances, I take an essential assumption of Kant's transcendental idealism to be that things-in-themselves exist. In other words, there is a reality independent of the human forms of cognition, especially of time and space.[145] What is at stake, however, is whether this mind-independent reality actually matches our idea-based projections of it.

With regard to the problem of truth-evaluation, this suggests that ideas used as *foci imaginarii* serve to project the *ultimate circumstances of evaluation* for our cognition. At these circumstances, the truth of our cognitions is assessed in

---

[144] An ideal is 'an individual thing which is determinable, or even determined, through the idea alone' (A568/B596).

[145] Kant provides other arguments for this assumption, and the *doctrinal-belief* interpretation of the supreme principle of reason, discussed in 1.5, might give a plausible account of such an argument. For other accounts, see Allison (2004), Allais (2015), and Stang (2016).

light of the states of the world that ultimately make our cognitions true.[146] These circumstances should thus be identified with the *world as it is in itself*, rather than the world of appearances, which is structured by the human forms of cognition and contingently carved up by empirical conceptualization (see 4.3 and 4.4). We may call this the world viewed 'from nowhere' or simply *without perspective*.[147] And this is the world we *should* aim to know.

To sum up, the transcendental deduction, whether successful or not, is meant to show that ideas of reason are 'legislative for us' (A695/B723): they define the 'indispensable standard for reason ... to assess and measure the degree and the defects of what is incomplete' in our cognition of nature (A569–570/B597–598). Ideas project an ultimate reality as the ideal standard of truth, which, because it is freed from the limitations of the human perspective, is normatively binding across all times and places, across all cognitive subjects and epistemic groups.[148] However, there is no a priori guarantee that the *actual process* of human inquiry will ever approximate this ideal standard.[149] It remains fundamentally open from the human standpoint what the human horizon actually converges upon, if it converges at all. We can only hope to approach a truthful description of nature by continuously refining and revising our empirical concepts and cognitions. We can only hope to reach the ultimate reality in the ideal limit of all our epistemic inquiries.[150]

One may object to the perspectivalist interpretation that it leaves the function of ideas fundamentally ambivalent: it seems unclear when an idea serves to outline the world of appearances as the context of intelligibility and when it serves to project ultimate reality as circumstances of evaluation. The fact, however, that one and the same idea serves both purposes is the key to resolving the impasse between fictionalism and noumenalism. The double function of ideas to delineate the human horizon and to project ideal standards of truth beyond the human horizon gives rise to our rational hope that the world of appearances, which is conditioned by human limits and contingent empirical

---

[146] Similarly, Melamedoff-Vosters (2022:43–46) conceives of things-in-themselves as truth-makers.

[147] See Nagel (1986). The perspectivalist view allows for the possibility that the world as such is conceived by a divine intellect.

[148] Massimi (2021:3291) offers an insightful interpretation of ideas, deployed as a *focus imaginarius*, for our understanding of scientific disagreement. An idea provides scientific communities with a 'shared conversational scoreboard', which serves as a common point of reference to resolve disagreement across times and across communities.

[149] Similarly, Kreines (2017) argues that laws of nature are unknowable from the empirical standpoint of finite cognizers.

[150] The perspectivalist view bears similarities with Kitcher's (1986) pragmatist interpretation of the idea of a systematically unified nature as the limit of an ideal inquiry. The view differs in that it incorporates a realist stance: it concedes the existence of a mind-independent world, but leaves its attainability at the limit unprovable.

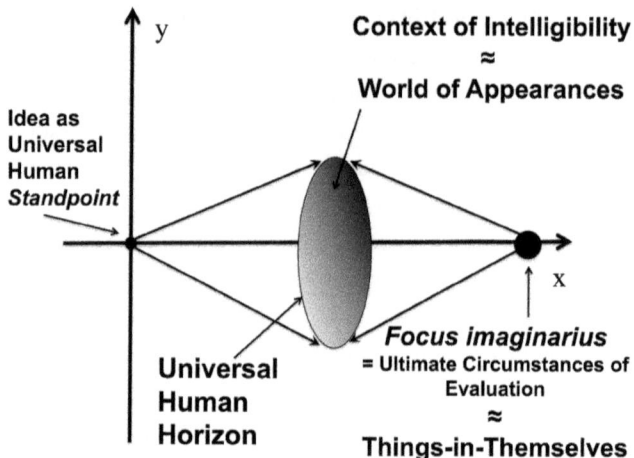

Figure 5 Schematic mapping of the world of appearances, i.e., the universal human horizon, and ultimate reality, i.e., the world without perspective or things-in-themselves, in the ideal limit of inquiry.

choices, will eventually converge with the world without perspective in the ideal limit of infinite inquiry. Figure 5 illustrates this mapping.[151] Without presupposing ideas of reason as objectively valid ideal standards of truth, nature could not be intelligible to us at all and cognition would lose its meaning for us. Such ideals cannot themselves be asserted as theoretical truths but must be presupposed in our human practice of exploring nature.

Conclusion

This Element has offered a perspectivalist interpretation of Kant's ideas of theoretical reason. The interpretation highlights how ideas mark the distinctively human standpoint and are indispensable for coping with the perspectival situatedness of our attempts to understand the world. The interpretation explains the transcendental role that these ideas have in empirical cognition of nature, while avoiding two temptations: the elevation of these ideas to the status of real

---

[151] This result is in line with Spohn's (2016:1357–1358) proposal that the two notions of *world* in his two-dimensional semantics correspond – with qualifications – to Kant's conception of the phenomenal and the noumenal world. On Spohn's view, there is the *totality of states of affairs* that we can describe by language (i.e., 'Wittgensteinian world', Spohn 2016:1343). This world corresponds to Kant's world of appearances. The epistemically possible worlds feature in the contents of our beliefs (i.e., 'Lewisian universes', Spohn 2016:1342). It is initially unknown in which universe we live, and we can only explore it gradually 'to its ideal limit' (Spohn 2016:1348–1349). Spohn (2016:1350–1353) concludes that a fundamental premise of two-dimensional semantics is that the world we describe by facts ultimately maps onto the actual Lewisian universe we live in.

things which exist in a metaphysically robust sense (as in noumenalism), and the reduction of these ideas to non-referring but pragmatically useful fictions (as in fictionalism). By assigning two essential functions to the regulative use of ideas in cognition, the perspectivalist interpretation can, however, reconcile both noumenalism and fictionalism.

First, ideas complement the semantic function of the understanding in determining objective content. In this function, an idea outlines the maximum field in which the understanding can progress towards a systematic unity of its use. The regulative use of an idea generates what I have called a context of intelligibility, that is, a kind of mental map of empirical reality as a structured whole. This is the context in which human experience is intelligible as sufficiently determined, inferentially related cognition of objects. From such a context, specific rules for the systematic use of the understanding in the outlined domain can be derived. The context that is presupposed in a particular experience defines the kind of object (i.e., natural kind) that can be cognized. Ideas in this semantic function guide a dynamic process of progressive determination of empirical concepts and cognitions within the *universal horizon of human understanding*.

Second, ideas provide normative standards for assessing the truth of empirical cognition. In this epistemic function, ideas as *foci imaginarii* project an ultimate reality in which all objects are completely determined. As such, ideas stand in for the ultimate circumstances of evaluation, that is, the states of the world that would make human cognition true. These circumstances can be identified with the world as it is in itself, independent of the human mind, or simply the *world without perspective*.

The perspectivalist interpretation resolves the impasse between noumenalism and fictionalism. It incorporates a moderate version of fictionalism that acknowledges the productive character of ideas by giving the world of appearances an a priori structure. There is, however, no time at which this world ever exists as a whole or is completely determined. From the standpoint of experience, the idea of nature as a whole must remain a heuristic fiction to guide the systematic use of the understanding. But it is not an empty fiction: it designates (in a weak sense) an empirical reality that is unfolding in time according to the idea. The perspectivalist interpretation is also compatible with a moderate version of noumenalism. It allows for the projection of a mind-independent world that serves as a normative ideal for truth-evaluation. Ideas direct the human mind towards an ultimate reality as the objective end of all human inquiry.

The perspectivalist interpretation thus qualifies the ontological commitments of each view: it is committed neither to the existence of real things that are referred to or accurately described by ideas, as is noumenalism, nor to the non-referential emptiness of ideas, as is fictionalism. It acknowledges that the wholes that ideas outline or project can never themselves be determined in truth-apt judgements, although such wholes must be presupposed for the very possibility of reference and truth-apt judgement. By contrast, noumenalism and fictionalism (in some versions) err precisely in committing themselves to the existence or, respectively, non-existence of such wholes as real things.

There remains a fundamental indeterminacy in Kant's doctrine of ideas, which the perspectivalist interpretation can embrace. It is fundamentally open whether the human horizon will converge upon the world without perspective at the ultimate end point of inquiry. Nonetheless, we must rationally hope that we live in a world that is intelligible to us and that, if we orient ourselves by rational guidelines, we will make real progress in our understanding of this world.

Abbreviations

In citing Kant's texts the following abbreviations are used:

- CPR   *Critique of Pure Reason* (1781/1787) (Ak., vols. 3–4) (see Primary Literature section)
- CJ   *Critique of the Power of Judgment* (1790) (Ak., vol. 5)
- DSS   *Dreams of a Spirit-Seer, Elucidated by Dreams of Metaphysics* (1766) (Ak., vol. 2)
- FI   *First Introduction to the Critique of the Power of Judgment* (Ak., vol. 20)
- JL   *Jäsche Logic* (1800) (Ak., vol. 9)
- Log-Bl   *Logic Blomberg* (Ak., vol. 24)
- Log-D   *Logic Dohna-Wundlacken* (1770s) (Ak., vol. 24)
- Log-W   *Logic Vienna* (1770s) (Ak., vol. 24)
- MFNS   *Metaphysical Foundations of Natural Science* (1786) (Ak., vol. 4)
- P   *Prolegomena to Any Future Metaphysics that Will Be Able to Come Forward As a Science* (1783) (Ak., vol. 4)

References

Primary Literature

All references are according to *Kant's gesammelte Schriften*, edited by the *Königlich Preußischen Akademie der Wissenschaften (Ak.)*, 29 vols. (Berlin: De Gruyter, 1902–). I usually provide the *Akademie* page number. With respect to the *Critique of Pure Reason*, I employ the standard A/B pagination.

English Translations

English translations are according to *The Cambridge Edition of the Works of Immanuel Kant*, edited by Paul Guyer and Allen Wood (Cambridge: Cambridge University Press, 1992–).

Kant, Immanuel (1998). *Critique of Pure Reason*. Guyer, Paul/Wood, Allen (trans.). Cambridge: Cambridge University Press.

Kant, Immanuel (2000). *Critique of the Power of Judgment*. Guyer, Paul/ Matthews, Eric (trans.). Cambridge: Cambridge University Press.

Kant, Immanuel (2003). *Theoretical Philosophy, 1755–1770*. Walford, David/ Meerbote, Ralf (trans.). Cambridge: Cambridge University Press.

Kant, Immanuel (2004). *Metaphysical Foundations of Natural Science*. Friedman, Michael (trans.). Cambridge: Cambridge University Press.

Kant, Immanuel (2004). *Lectures on Logic*. Young, J. Michael (trans.). Cambridge: Cambridge University Press.

Kant, Immanuel (2010). *Theoretical Philosophy after 1781*. Allison, Henry E./ Heath, Peter/Hatfield, Gary/Friedman, Michael (trans.). Cambridge: Cambridge University Press.

Further Literature

Abela, Paul (2006). 'The Demands of Systematicity: Rational Judgment and the Structure of Nature'. In Graham Bird (ed.) *A Companion to Kant*. Oxford: Blackwell, pp. 408–422.

Adickes, Erich (1924). *Kant und das Ding an sich*. Berlin: Verlag Rolf Heise.

Adickes, Erich (1927). *Kant und die Als-Ob-Philosophie*. Stuttgart: Frommans Verlag.

Allais, Lucy (2015). *Manifest Reality: Kant's Idealism and his Realism*. New York: Oxford University Press.

Allison, Henry E. (2004). *Kant's Transcendental Idealism: An Interpretation and Defense; Revised and Enlarged Edition*. New Haven: Yale University Press.

References

Ameriks, Karl (2003). *Interpreting Kant's Critiques*. New York: Oxford University Press.
Ameriks, Karl (2006). 'A Common-Sense Kant?'. In Karl Ameriks (ed.) *Kant and the Historical Turn*. New York: Oxford University Press, pp. 108–133.
Anderson, R. Lanier (2014). *The Poverty of Conceptual Truth: Kant's Analytic/Synthetic Distinction and the Limits of Metaphysics*. Oxford: Oxford University Press.
Bacon, Francis (1620/2012). *New Organon, or True Directions Concerning the Interpretation of Nature*. Cambridge: Cambridge University Press.
Baumgarten, Alexander G. (1750/1758). *Aesthetica*. Frankfurt an der Oder: G. Olms.
Breitenbach, Angela (2014). 'Biological Purposiveness and Analogical Reflection'. In Ina Goy and Eric Watkins (eds.) *Kant's Theory of Biology*. Berlin: De Gruyter, pp. 131–148.
Buchdahl, Gerd (1967). 'The Relation between "Understanding" and "Reason"'. *Proceedings of the Aristotelian Society*, 67, 209–226.
Buchdahl, Gerd (1969). *Metaphysics and the Philosophy of Science. The Classical Origins: Descartes to Kant*. Oxford: Basil Blackwell.
Buchdahl, Gerd (1971). 'The Conception of Lawlikeness in Kant's Philosophy of Science'. *Synthese*, 23(1), 24–46.
Callanan, John (2021). 'The Boundary of Pure Reason'. In Peter Thielke (ed.) *Kant's Prolegomena*. Cambridge: Cambridge University Press, pp. 133–153.
Cassirer, Ernst (1999). *Das Erkenntnisproblem in der Philosophie und Wissenschaft der neueren Zeit. Zweiter Band*. In Birgit Recki (ed.) *Gesammelte Werke*. Hamburger Ausgabe. Band 3. Hamburg: Meiner.
Chaplin, Rosalind (2024). 'Kant on the Conceptual Possibility of Actually Infinite *Tota Synthetica*'. *Kantian Review*, https://doi.org/10.1017/S1369415424 000220.
Chignell, Andrew (2007a). 'Belief in Kant'. *The Philosophical Review*, 116(3), 323–360.
Chignell, Andrew (2007b). 'Kant's Concepts of Justification'. *Noûs*, 41(1), 33–63.
Chignell, Andrew (2014). 'Modal Motivations for Noumenal Ignorance: Knowledge, Cognition, and Coherence'. *Kant-Studien*, 105(4), 573–597.
Caimi, Mario (1995). 'Über eine wenig beachtete Deduktion der regulativen Ideen'. *Kant-Studien*, 86(3), 308–320.
Dyck, Corey (2014). *Kant and Rational Psychology*. Oxford: Oxford University Press.
Falkenburg, Brigitte (2020). *Kant's Cosmology: From the Pre-Critical System to the Antinomy of Pure Reason*. Berlin: Springer.

Fichte, Johann G. (1796–1799). *Wissenschaftslehre nova methodo*. In Reinhard Lauth, Hans Jacobs, Hans Gliwitzky, and Eric Fuchts (eds.) *J. G. Fichte: Gesamtausgabe der Bayerischen Akademie der Wissenschaften*. Volume IV, Stuttgart-Bad Cannstatt: Frommann, 1964–.

Friedman, Michael (2013). *Kant's Construction of Nature: A Reading of the Metaphysical Foundations of Natural Science*. Cambridge: Cambridge University Press.

Frierson, Patrick (2022). 'What is the Idea of the Soul? Comments on Katharina Kraus, *Kant on Self-Knowledge and Self-Formation*'. *Kantian Review*, 27(3), 475–481.

Gadamer, Hans-Georg (1960). *Wahrheit und Methode*. Tübingen: Mohr Siebeck.

Geiger, Ido (2003) 'Is the Assumption of a Systematic Whole of Empirical Concepts a Necessary Condition of Knowledge?' *Kant-Studien*, 94(3), 273–298.

Geiger, Ido (2022). *Kant and the Claims of the Empirical World: A Transcendental Reading of the* Critique of the Power of Judgment. Cambridge: Cambridge University Press.

Gerson, Lloyd (2013). *From Plato to Platonism*. Ithaca: Cornell University Press.

Ginsborg, Hannah (2006). 'Empirical Concepts and the Content of Experience'. *European Journal of Philosophy*, 14(3), 349–372.

Ginsborg, Hannah (2017). 'Why Must We Presuppose the Systematicity of Nature?' In Michela Massimi and Angela Breitenbach (eds.) *Kant and the Laws of Nature*. Cambridge: Cambridge University Press, pp. 71–88.

Grier, Michelle (1997). 'Kant on the Illusion of a Systematic Unity of Knowledge'. *History of Philosophy Quarterly*, 14, 1–28.

Grier, Michelle (2001). *Kant's Doctrine of Transcendental Illusion*. Cambridge: Cambridge University Press.

Guyer, Paul (1979). *Kant and the Claims of Taste*. Cambridge: Cambridge University Press.

Guyer, Paul (1990). 'Reason and Reflective Judgment: Kant on the Significance of Systematicity'. *Noûs*, 24, 17–43.

Guyer, Paul (2003). 'Kant on the Systematicity of Nature: Two Puzzles'. *History of Philosophy Quarterly*, 20(3), 277–295.

Hegel, Georg W. F. (1807). *Phänomenologie des Geistes*. Translated as *Phenomenology of Spirit*, by Terry Pinkard. Cambridge: Cambridge University Press, 2017.

Heidegger, Martin (1927). *Sein und Zeit*. Translated as *Being and Time*, by John Macquarrie and Edward Robinson. Oxford: Basil Blackwell, 1962.

Hoffer, Noam (2019). 'Kant's Regulative Metaphysics of God and the Lawfulness of Nature'. *The Southern Journal of Philosophy*, 57(2), 217–239.

Hoffer, Noam (2023). 'Kant's Regulative Essentialism and the Unknowability of Real Essences'. *European Journal of Philosophy*, 31(4), 887–901.

Hogan, Desmond (2009). 'How to Know Unknowable Things in Themselves'. *Noûs*, 43(1), 49–63.

Hogan, Desmond (2021). 'Handedness, Idealism, and Freedom'. *The Philosophical Review*, 130(3), 385–449.

Howard, Stephen (2022a). 'Kant on Limits, Boundaries, and the Positive Function of Ideas'. *European Journal of Philosophy*, 30(1), 64–78.

Howard, Stephen (2022b). 'From the Boundary of the World to the Boundary of Reason: The First Antinomy and the Development of Kant's Critical Philosophy'. *HOPOS: The Journal of the International Society for the History of Philosophy of Science*, 12(1), 225–241.

Howard, Stephen (2024). 'The Cosmological Ideas in Kant's Critical Philosophy: Their Unique Status and Twofold Regulative Use'. *The Southern Journal of Philosophy*, https://doi.org/10.1111/sjp.12529.

Hume, David (1748/2007). *An Enquiry Concerning Human Understanding*. Cambridge: Cambridge University Press.

Husserl, Edmund (1900). *Logische Untersuchungen. Erster Band: Prolegomena zur reinen Logik*. In Edmund Holenstein (ed.) *Husserliana XVIII*. The Hague: Nijhoff, 1975.

Kaplan, David (1989). 'Demonstratives'. In Joseph Almog, John Perry, and Howard Wettstein (eds.) *Themes from Kaplan*. New York: Oxford University Press, pp. 481–563.

Kitcher, Philip (1986). 'Projecting the Order of Nature'. In Robert Butts (ed.) *Kant's Philosophy of Physical Science*. Dordrecht: Reidel, pp. 201–235.

Kraus, Katharina (2018). 'The Soul as the "Guiding Idea" of Psychology: Kant on Scientific Psychology, Systematicity, and the Idea of the Soul'. *Studies in History and Philosophy of Science*, 71, 77–88.

Kraus, Katharina (2020). *Kant on Self-Knowledge and Self-Formation. The Nature of Inner Experience*. Cambridge: Cambridge University Press.

Kraus, Katharina (2022). 'Précis of *Kant on Self-Knowledge and Self-Formation* and Replies to Critics'. *Kantian Review*, 27(3), 491–508.

Kraus, Katharina (2023). 'Contemporary Kantian Philosophy of Science'. In Sorin Baiasu and Mark Timmons (eds.) *The Kantian Mind*. London: Routledge, pp. 568–580.

Kreines, James (2009). 'Kant on the Laws of Nature and the Limitations of our Knowledge'. *European Journal of Philosophy*, 17(4), 527–558.

Kreines, James (2017). 'Kant on the Laws of Nature: Restrictive Inflationism and Its Philosophical Advantages'. *The Monist*, 100(3), 326–341.

Leibniz, Gottfried W. (1693). *De L'Horizon de la Doctrine Humaine*. La Restitution Universelle (Bibliotheque Des Textes Philosophiques). Paris: Vrin (1991).

Lewis, David (1980). 'Index, Context, and Content'. In Stig Kanger and Sven Öhman (eds.) *Philosophy and Grammar*. Dordrecht: Reidel, pp. 79–100.

Longuenesse, Béatrice (1998). *Kant and the Capacity to Judge*. Princeton: Princeton University Press.

Longuenesse, Béatrice (2005). *Kant on the Human Standpoint*. Cambridge: Cambridge University Press.

Makkreel, Rudolf (1990). *Imagination and Interpretation in Kant: The Hermeneutical Import of the* Critique of Judgment. Chicago: University of Chicago Press.

Maly, Sebastian (2011). *Kant über die symbolische Erkenntnis Gottes*. Berlin: De Gruyter.

Massimi, Michela (2017). 'What Is This Thing Ccalled "Scientific Knowledge"? Kant on Imaginary Standpoints and the Regulative Role of Reason'. *Kant Yearbook*, 9, 63–83.

Massimi, Michela (2021). 'Points of View. Kant on Perspectival Knowledge'. *Synthese* (Supplement 13), 198, 3279–3296.

Massimi, Michela and Breitenbach, Angela (eds.) (2017). *Kant and the Laws of Nature*. Cambridge: Cambridge University Press.

McDowell, John (1994). *Mind and World*. Cambridge, MA: Harvard University Press.

McLaughlin, Peter (2014). 'Transcendental Presuppositions and Ideas of Reason'. *Kant-Studien*, 105(4), 554–572.

McNulty, Michael B. (2015). 'Rehabilitating the Regulative Use of Reason: Kant on Empirical and Chemical Laws'. *Studies in History and Philosophy of Science* (Part A), 54, 1–10.

Meier, Georg F. (1752). *Vernunftlehre*. Halle: J. J. Gebauer.

Melamedoff-Vosters, Damian (2022). 'Truthmaker Noumenalism'. *Australasian Journal of Philosophy*, 100(1), 40–55.

Nagel, Thomas (1986). *The View from Nowhere*. Oxford: Oxford University Press.

Nassar, Dalia (2016). 'Analogical Reflection As a Source for the Science of Life: Kant and the Possibility of the Biological Sciences'. *Studies in History and Philosophy of Science*, 58, 57–66.

O'Shea, James (1997). 'The needs of the Understanding: Kant on Empirical Laws and Regulative Ideals'. *International Journal of Philosophical Studies*, 5, 216–254.

Pickering, Marc (2016). 'Kant's Theoretical Reasons for Belief in Things in Themselves'. *Kant-Studien*, 107(4), 589–616.

Proops, Ian (2021). *The Fiery Test of Critique: A Reading of Kant's Dialectic*. Oxford: Oxford University Press.

Posy, Carl (1981). 'The Language of Appearances and Things in Themselves'. *Synthese*, 47(2), 313–352.

Posy, Carl (1983). 'Dancing to the Antinomy: A Proposal for Transcendental Idealism'. *American Philosophical Quarterly*, 20(1), 81–94.

Ritter, Joachim, Hinske, Norbert, Engfer, Hans Jurgen, Janssen, Paul, and Scherner, Maximilian (1974). 'Horizont'. In Joachim Ritter (ed.) *Historisches Wörterbuch der Philosophie* Vol. 3. Stuttgart: Schwabe Verlag, pp. 1188–1206.

Rohlf, Michael (2010). 'The Ideas of Pure Reason'. In Paul Guyer (ed.) *Cambridge Companion to Immanuel Kant's* Critique of Pure Reason. Cambridge: Cambridge University Press, pp. 190–209.

Rosefeldt, Tobias (2021). 'Kant on Decomposing Synthesis and the Intuition of Infinite Space'. *Philosophers' Imprint*, 22(1), 1–23.

Rush, Fred (2000) 'Reason and Regulation in Kant'. *Review of Metaphysics*, 53(4), 837–862.

Schafer, Karl (2023). *Kant's Reason: The Unity of Reason and the Limits of Comprehension in Kant*. New York: Oxford University Press.

Spagnesi, Lorenzo (2022). 'The Idea of God and the Investigation of Nature in Kant's Transcendental Dialectic'. *Kantian Review*, 27(2), 279–297.

Spagnesi, Lorenzo (2023a). 'A Rule-Based Account of the Regulative Use of Reason in Kant's *Critique of Pure Reason*'. *European Journal of Philosophy*, 31(3), 673–688.

Spagnesi, Lorenzo (2023b). 'The Systematic Unity of Reason and Empirical Truth in Kant's *Critique of Pure Reason*'. *Kant-Studien*, 114(3), 435–462.

Spohn, Wolfgang (2016). 'Three Kinds of Worlds and Two Kinds of Truth'. *Philosophical Studies*, 173(5), 1335–1359.

Stang, Nicholas (2016). *Kant's Modal Metaphysics*. New York: Oxford University Press.

Stang, Nicholas (forthcoming). 'Why Should Metaphysics be Systematic? Contemporary Answers and Kant's'. In Aaron Segal and Nicholas Stang (eds.) *Systematic Metaphysics: Historical and Contemporary Perspectives*. Oxford: Oxford University Press.

Stevenson, Leslie (2003). 'Opinion, Belief or Faith, and Knowledge'. *Kantian Review*, 7, 72–101.

Sturm, Thomas (2009). *Kant und die Wissenschaften vom Menschen*. Paderborn: Mentis.

Vaihinger, Hans (1911). *Die Philosophie des Als Ob. System der theoretischen, praktischen und religiösen Fiktionen der Menschheit auf Grund eines idealistischen Positivismus: Mit einem Anhang über Kant und Nietzsche*. Berlin: Reuther & Reichard.

Van Inwagen, Peter (2008). *Metaphysics: An Introduction*. 3rd ed. Philadelphia: Westview Press.

Watkins, Eric (2013). 'Kant on *Infima Species*'. In Alfredo Ferrarin, Claudio La Rocca, and Margit Ruffing (eds.) *Kant und die Philosophie in weltbürgerlicher Absicht: Akten des XI. Internationalen Kant-Kongresses*. Berlin: De Gruyter, pp. 283–296.

Watkins, Eric (2016). 'The Unconditioned and the Absolute in Kant and Early German Romanticism'. *Kant Yearbook*, 8(1), 117–42.

Watkins, Eric (2019a). *Kant on Laws*. Cambridge: Cambridge University Press.

Watkins, Eric (2019b). 'Kant on Real Conditions'. In Violette L. Waibel and Margit Ruffing (eds.) *Proceedings of the XII. International Kant Congress Nature and Freedom*. Berlin: De Gruyte, pp. 1133–1140.

Watkins, Eric and Willaschek, Marcus (2017). 'Kant's Account of Cognition'. *Journal of the History of Philosophy*, 55(1), 83–112.

Watkins, Eric and Willaschek, Marcus (2020). 'Kant on Cognition and Knowledge'. *Synthese*, 197, 3195–3213.

Willaschek, Marcus (2018). *Kant on the Sources of Metaphysics: The Dialectic of Pure Reason*. Cambridge: Cambridge University Press.

Wuerth, Julian (2014). *Kant on Mind, Action, and Ethics*. Oxford: Oxford University Press.

Ypi, Lea (2021). *The Architectonic of Reason: Purposiveness and Systematic Unity in Kant's* Critique of Pure Reason. Oxford: Oxford University Press.

Zuckert, Rachel (2007). *Kant on Beauty and Biology: An Interpretation of the* Critique of Judgement. Cambridge: Cambridge University Press.

Zuckert, Rachel (2017). 'Empirical Scientific Investigation and the Ideas of Reason' In Michela Massimi and Angela Breitenbach (eds.) *Kant and the Laws of Nature*. Cambridge: Cambridge University Press, pp. 89–107.

Zuckert, Rachel (2020). 'Attempting to Exit the Human Perspective: A Priori Experimentation in Kant's *Critique of Pure Reason*'. In Ana-Maria Crețu and Michela Massimi (eds.) *Knowledge from a Human Point of View*. Berlin: Springer, pp. 1–18.

Acknowledgements

The perspectivalist interpretation I develop in this Element was motivated by my earlier research on Kant's idea of the soul (Kraus 2020) and has been inspired by numerous personal conversations as well as questions and discussions after talks in which I presented versions of this view. I am deeply indebted to the community of Kant scholars and to colleagues in other areas of philosophy with whom I have had the privilege and pleasure of testing my reading. I thank Desmond Hogan, editor of this Element series, for inviting me to write on this topic. For detailed and helpful comments on earlier versions of this manuscript, I am especially grateful to Garrath Williams, Aaron Wells, Eric Watkins, Lorenzo Spagnesi, Reverend Philip-Neri Reese O.P., Desmond Hogan, Christopher Benzenberg, Karl Ameriks, and an anonymous reviewer. For valuable feedback on the project, I also thank Lucy Allais, Robert Audi, Martin Baesler, Patricia Blanchette, Jochen Bojanowski, Rodrigo Zanette de Araujo, Jenann Ismael, Anja Jauernig, Béatrice Longuenesse, Tobias Rosefeldt, Fred Rush, Jeff Speaks, audiences in Berlin, Leuven, Mainz, New York, Tel Aviv, and Tübingen as well as the participants of the Johns Hopkins Workshop in the History of Philosophy. Last but not least, I am extremely grateful to Benjamin Wallach and Austin Wang for their diligent editorial help in finalizing this manuscript. I also thank Andy Jones and the team at Cambridge University Press for their excellent assistance and advice.

Acknowledgments

Cambridge Elements

The Philosophy of Immanuel Kant

Desmond Hogan
Princeton University

Desmond Hogan joined the philosophy department at Princeton in 2004. His interests include Kant, Leibniz and German rationalism, early modern philosophy, and questions about causation and freedom. Recent work includes 'Kant on the Foreknowledge of Contingent Truths', *Res Philosophica* 91(1) (2014); 'Kant's Theory of Divine and Secondary Causation', in Brandon Look (ed.) *Leibniz and Kant*, Oxford University Press (2021); 'Kant and the Character of Mathematical Inference', in Carl Posy and Ofra Rechter (eds.) *Kant's Philosophy of Mathematics Vol. I*, Cambridge University Press (2020).

Howard Williams
University of Cardiff

Howard Williams was appointed Honorary Distinguished Professor at the Department of Politics and International Relations, University of Cardiff in 2014. He is also Emeritus Professor in Political Theory at the Department of International Politics, Aberystwyth University, a member of the Coleg Cymraeg Cenedlaethol (Welsh-language national college) and a Fellow of the Learned Society of Wales. He is the author of *Marx* (1980); *Kant's Political Philosophy* (1983); *Concepts of Ideology* (1988); *Hegel, Heraclitus and Marx's Dialectic* (1989); *International Relations in Political Theory* (1992); *International Relations and the Limits of Political Theory* (1996); *Kant's Critique of Hobbes: Sovereignty and Cosmopolitanism* (2003); *Kant and the End of War* (2012) and is currently editor of the journal Kantian Review. He is writing a book on the Kantian legacy in political philosophy for a new series edited by Paul Guyer.

Allen Wood
Indiana University

Allen Wood is Ward W. and Priscilla B. Woods Professor Emeritus at Stanford University. He was a John S. Guggenheim Fellow at the Free University in Berlin, a National Endowment for the Humanities Fellow at the University of Bonn and Isaiah Berlin Visiting Professor at the University of Oxford. He is on the editorial board of eight philosophy journals, five book series and The Stanford Encyclopedia of Philosophy. Along with Paul Guyer, Professor Wood is co-editor of The Cambridge Edition of the Works of Immanuel Kant and translator of the Critique of Pure Reason. He is the author or editor of a number of other works, mainly on Kant, Hegel and Karl Marx. His most recently published books are *Fichte's Ethical Thought*, Oxford University Press (2016) and *Kant and Religion*, Cambridge University Press (2020). Wood is a member of the American Academy of Arts and Sciences.

About the Series

This Cambridge Elements series provides an extensive overview of Kant's philosophy and its impact upon philosophy and philosophers. Distinguished Kant specialists provide an up-to-date summary of the results of current research in their fields and give their own take on what they believe are the most significant debates influencing research, drawing original conclusions.

Cambridge Elements

The Philosophy of Immanuel Kant

Elements in the Series

Kant and the French Revolution
Reidar Maliks

The Kantian Federation
Luigi Caranti

The Politics of Beauty: A Study of Kant's Critique of Taste
Susan Meld Shell

Kant's Theory of Labour
Jordan Pascoe

Kant's Late Philosophy of Nature: The Opus postumum
Stephen Howard

Kant on Freedom
Owen Ware

Kant on Self-Control
Marijana Vujošević

Kant on Rational Sympathy
Benjamin Vilhauer

The Moral Foundation of Right
Paul Guyer

The Postulate of Public Right
Patrick Capps and Julian Rivers

Kant on the History and Development of Practical Reason
Olga Lenczewska

Kant's Ideas of Reason
Katharina T. Kraus

A full series listing is available at: www.cambridge.org/EPIK

For EU product safety concerns, contact us at Calle de José Abascal, 56–1°,
28003 Madrid, Spain or eugpsr@cambridge.org.